TIME MANAGEMENT
GOD's WAY

TIME MANAGEMENT GOD's WAY

GLORIA ADAMS

TIME MANAGEMENT GOD'S WAY
Copyright © 2007 Gloria Adams

ISBN 978-1-886068-16-2
Library of Congress Control Number: 2006938883
Christian Life • Religious and Inspirational
Personal Growth • Faith • Self-Help

Published by Fruitbearer Publishing
P.O. Box 777, Georgetown, DE 19947 • (302) 856-6649 • FAX (302) 856-7742
www.fruitbearer.com • fruitbearer.publishing@verizon.net

Cover design by Carmelle Scott, Longtail Graphics

Printed in the United States of America

ACKNOWLEDGMENTS

Special Thanks . . .

To my sister, Jacquie Martin, for typing most of my manuscript and encouraging me to trust God to start my assignment—to write this book by faith.

To Rev. Lonnie Henderson for your review of my manuscript to make sure that I was rightly dividing the Word of God for sound doctrine.

To Sister Angie Terrell for your precious time to edit my manuscript as a first-time writer, encouraging me to continue to write.

To Carmelle Scott for capturing the vision for the cover of the book.

To my parents, James and Mary Harris, for encouraging me to become all that God is calling me to be in Christ Jesus.

To my daughters, Selena Adams and Shante Carter, for allowing me to share my faith with you and to model Christ before you.

To my son-in-law, Aaron Carter, and my granddaughter, Zoe Carter; you are a part of my family. Now I get to share my faith with you and model Christ before you.

To my family, friends, and church family, Celebration Church, for your love, support and prayers, as you prayed me through to complete this book.

To my publisher, Candy Abbott, for your sensitivity to the voice of the Lord and for publishing God's message to His people.

TABLE OF CONTENTS

INTRODUCTION

Are you managing your time the way that God designed it especially for you?

Everyone is given the same number of hours in the day, but the way the time is used varies from person to person. God has given each of us a custom-fit blueprint for how we should live our lives. Jeremiah 29:11 says that God knows the plans that He has for us: ". . . plans to prosper and not to harm [us], plans to give [us] a hope and a future." God wants us to use our time to live a prosperous and good life that is full of hope. We can have this kind of life if we as children of God allow our heavenly Father to manage our time for us according to His perfect will. How can we know His will for our lives? We need to seek Him first and know His Word, which will govern our lives as we yield to His lordship.

Even though there are many secular books out there that tell us how to manage our time, God wants to tell us how to manage our time from *His* perspective because He has a special plan designed for our individual lives. Are we allowing God to provide our daily agenda to fulfill those plans that He has for us? With God's plans, we will prosper and not be harmed, as well as experiencing boundless hope for our lives. God already has plans for our personal time management so that we can fulfill His purposes and attain our destiny in Christ Jesus.

Are you fulfilling your destiny that God has created for you before the foundations of the world? Have you ever stopped and thought, *Where is the time going? I need more time! I need time to finish my project—the one that only I can do—or the ministry that God has called me to do, but I don't have enough time to do it. What happened to the time?*

One morning, I woke up feeling the urge to seize the time because I felt that it was slipping away from me. I was sad for a moment, but then I thought that I still had enough time in the day. I immediately pressed into a place of prayer with God and began to worship Him for who He is. Then, I spent a quiet time with God, needing Him to minister to me because I felt that I had missed out by not doing some of the things that He called me to do. Sensing God's presence, I felt Him ministering to me with a reminder that I still had enough time that day to find out from Him what I needed to do. He also prompted me not to waste any more time thinking about the time that I had already wasted, but to use the time that I had left to accomplish what He created me for. As my foundation for *Time Management God's Way*, God directed my attention to Matthew 6:33, which says, "But seek ye first the kingdom of God and his righteousness, and all these things shall be added unto you" (KJV).

God wanted me to let Him manage my time by giving it back to Him so that He could multiply it back to me. In turn, I could invest my time back into His kingdom. God promised me that if I entrusted my time to Him to do what He called me to do, then He would meet all my needs, and the Holy Spirit would guide me into all the truth necessary to live a successful life, full of boundless hope in Christ Jesus. Because my hope is in Christ Jesus, I chose to apply the biblical principle of sowing and reaping in Matthew 6:33 to help me manage my time.

If you are challenged by the concept of managing your time in an effective way, ask yourself if you're allowing God to manage your time. Are you investing your time in His kingdom doing what He created you to do, or are you managing your time doing what you choose to do without consulting the giver of time— God Himself? I hope that after reading this book, you will re-evaluate your management of time to see if you are seeking God's way of living or your own way of living. Proverbs 14:12 says that there is a way which seems right to a man or woman and it appears straight before him, but the end of it is the way of death. It can be the death of a dream, a vision, a successful and prosperous life, or, for some, death without the promise of eternal life with Christ Jesus.

In other words, how we spend our lives here on earth will determine how we spend our lives in eternity.

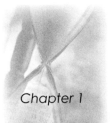

Chapter 1

WHAT IS
TIME MANAGEMENT GOD'S WAY?

Time is a precious commodity. Unfortunately, we cannot create more time or save it to spend on another day. Each person has exactly the same number of hours and minutes every day. The good news is that this is the day that the Lord has made, so rejoice and be glad in it (Psalm 118:24)!

It is good to know that I do not have to waste time thinking about the time I've already lost. I have not always realized how precious time is, but now that I am getting older, I am much more aware of my personal time management.

During one of my times of refreshing with the Lord, He revealed to me that I was not doing all that He created me to do. I was doing all the things that were important to me, but not to Him. The Lord pointed out to me that I was spiritually lazy in certain areas of my life, resulting in mismanagement of my time. There have been times that the Lord has placed on my heart certain things when He desired for me to do—only for me to put them off until later or never to do them at all.

I had to ask myself these questions: Was it because I did not know how to do these things? Was it a fear of failure or fear of success that was hindering me from doing these things? Perhaps it was my lack of faith that kept me from doing what He called me to do. All of these issues at one time or another deterred me from moving from a passive state to one of action. I could sense the Lord saying to me, "It is time for you to do what I created you to do."

God was making it clear to me that He gives us time as a gift—not to be used on ourselves—but to do His will. God was asking me what I did with my time. One particular question got my attention: was I managing time my way or God's way?

My way of managing time did not even come close to measuring up to His way. According to Jeremiah 29:11, the Lord already has plans for our time that will lead us to live prosperous and successful lives. He has given each one of us a certain lifespan to achieve our destiny, and He is the only one who knows when our time is up. Ecclesiastes 3:2 says there is a time to live and a time to die. God is the only one who is in control of both and everything in between.

God has our best interests at heart by wanting us to succeed. When I acknowledge God's sovereignty as the Creator of all things, the Alpha and Omega, the beginning and the end, why then should I not manage my time His way and yield my way to Him as the right way of doing things? *Time Management God's Way* involves allowing God to manage our time according to the plans He has for our individual lives.

The Lord placed on my heart that what I needed to do the most is spend time with Him to understand His agenda and strategy for managing my time. I made a decision to spend quality time with the Lord in prayer and meditation, listening to discover how He desires to manage my time. I've learned that when we place our time in God's hands, we are actually sowing our time back into God's kingdom, so we will reap the harvest of time multiplied back to us. This principle of sowing and reaping is found in Galatians 6:7: "A man reaps what he sows."

God reminded me that too often when this time is multiplied back to us, we misuse it for our own needs instead of investing it back into His kingdom. Many of us will use this increase in time to possess, accumulate, and acquire more things. The key to *Time Management God's Way* is that when we receive this increase in time, we will not use it for ourselves because that's selfish. (Self always seeks to be satisfied with everything except the things of God.) Instead, we should sow this increase of time back into God's kingdom.

Time Management God's Way alleviates stress in our lives by showing us how to yield our right-of-way to the Lord's way of living. God desires for us to use His strategy of time management to carry out the plans He has for our lives so that we will develop a single-minded focus on kingdom living.

The Lord impressed upon my heart that this was an important subject to be addressed because the signs of our Lord's imminent return are evident. In the meantime, we have vital work to do for His kingdom, so many of us should re-evaluate how we manage our time to see if we are investing it to advance His kingdom. These pages offer a challenge for us to take a closer look to see if we are managing our time His way or the world's way. God's way is higher than ours because He already knows the beginning and the end. His way will require us to put Him first in order of importance for everything that we do.

Each one of us will have to give an account of how we used our time while we were on the earth. Unfortunately, however, many of us are letting time slip by without doing what God created us to do. Remember that God is the only one who knows how much time we have on earth to accomplish all the plans that He has for our lives—not our plans, but *His* plans.

Time Management God's Way is about seeking to make the kingdom of God and His righteousness a priority in our lives. The following chapters will give us insight into seeking God's kingdom and His righteousness first, which will result in stress-free living.

Chapter 2

Seeking Both the Kingdom of God and His Righteousness

God gave me instructions for writing this book to explain the foundational Scripture, Matthew 6:33, so people will understand the importance of seeking both the kingdom of God and His righteousness and its impact on the concept of *Time Management God's Way*. This verse says, "But seek ye first the kingdom of God and his righteousness, and all these things shall be added to you" (KJV).

When we seek the kingdom of God first, we will have what we need. God wants us to be content with His way of life, which allows us to develop a single-minded focus on His kingdom and His righteousness. As a result, we will reap a harvest of blessings added to our lives by God's supernatural power, enabling us to have more time to do all that He is calling us to do.

I choose to manage my time God's way and not the world's way so that time will serve me instead of me serving time. God is always ready to bless us with more time to give us an abundant life. John 10:10 says, "The thief comes only to steal and kill and destroy; I have come that they may have life, and have it to the full."

Jesus came to earth to give us this full life *now;* we don't have to wait until we get to heaven to receive it. For born-again believers, the kingdom of God truly means "heaven on earth." We can experience abundant life now, but it will cost us time spent with God, who is the giver of time.

Let's take a closer look at the word "seek" in Matthew 6:33. It comes from the Greek word *zeteo,* which means to worship, to endeavor, or to earnestly seek after. It is a matter of hungering or desiring; it is to seek with a desire to worship. This implies that we should earnestly seek to worship God with our entire selves. According to Romans 12:1, we should offer our bodies "as living sacrifices, holy and pleasing to God—this is [our] spiritual act of worship." God desires for us to earnestly seek His kingdom and His righteousness in order for us to live our lives according to His kingdom values. We also should seek both the kingdom of God and His righteousness with perseverance until we obtain them: casual seeking will just not do.

The Lord desires for us to make Him our priority so that we can receive the blessings of heavenly provision. To further understand how to seek God's kingdom and His righteousness, let's look at verse 33 in the context of the passage. Matthew 6:31-32 says, "Therefore take no thought, saying, What shall we eat? or, What shall we drink? or, Wherewithal shall we be clothed? (For after all these things do the Gentiles seek) for your heavenly Father knoweth that ye have need of all these things" (KJV).

Epizeteo, another Greek word for "seek" used in verse 32, means to crave with an intense demand or to seek with much eagerness or with much stress. Jesus points out that the Gentiles eagerly seek after taking care of their material needs without understanding the Lord's provisional care. The word "Gentile" comes from the Greek word *ethnos,* which means "heathen" or "unbeliever." God does not want us to "seek" like the unbelievers who are filled with anxiety and stress because they choose not to surrender themselves to His care. The

Gentiles make it their priority to seek after temporal things instead of the kingdom of God, which is righteousness, peace, and joy in the Holy Spirit.

Time Management God's Way will empower us to enjoy stress-free lives when we live them according to God's kingdom values rather than the world's values. If we're striving for either set of values, then we will have them. Those who focus their attention on worldly things will receive their reward while they're living on the earth. As believers, however, we should be investing our time and energy in an eternal reward in heaven by putting God first in our lives.

The word "first" in the phrase, "Seek ye first the kingdom of God and His righteousness," comes from the Greek word, *protone*, which means "first, chief of all, or holding the highest place in our affections." In other words, the first place of our affections must revolve around the will of God. When we use the time given to us by God to do His will, we do not have to struggle to manage our time striving for material things. God promises that He will provide all of our necessities in this life; He will meet all our needs "according to His glorious riches in Christ Jesus" (Philippians 4:19).

We can manage our time better when we are not struggling to provide for all of our material things, which only brings anxiety to our minds. When we use this time to sow back into God's kingdom, however, God will return that time back to us. Sometimes we get this time multiplied back to us, only for us to use this time for ourselves: we seek after pleasure because the world system baits us with its appeal to the flesh. God wants for us to receive more time so that we can sow it back into His kingdom and the things of God. If we choose to invest this time in ourselves, then we will become focused on self rather than on God, which, in turn, could lead us to seeking the wrong goals in life that would rob us of precious time.

When we spend our time seeking God first along with His kingdom and righteousness, then we will make it our top priority to walk in obedient submission to His sovereign reign. God will honor our time by multiplying it, protecting it, and using it for His kingdom work. Some of us are using our moments just to satisfy the cravings of the sinful nature, instead of investing them back into the kingdom of God. Once we start feeding the flesh what it desires, nothing can satisfy that lust; subsequently, we stop making "seeking the kingdom of God and His righteousness" the first priority in our lives.

Matthew 6:33 is clear about what God's priority is for us: to seek first the kingdom of God and His righteousness. Then, He will add those things that He knows that we need. The word "add" comes from the Greek word *prostithemi*, which implies giving more than what we have. That is what God does when we put our time into His hands to do the work of His kingdom. Because God created us to live in both the spiritual (supernatural) and the natural realms, He will give us not only those things that are eternal, but also those things that we need while we live on earth. God's spiritual kingdom encompasses the hearts of born-again believers who live their lives according to Jesus' righteous standards.

God demands that His kingdom and His righteousness be the top priority in our lives, ahead of all our personal needs and interests. We must always be careful not to allow other things to compete with the things that are important to Him. In this world, our natural instinct is to seek after happiness, satisfaction, and self-gratification.

King Solomon experienced wealth, power, honor, fame, and sensual pleasure—only to find out that it all was meaningless. In his first-hand testimony in Ecclesiastes, he wrote that, in the end, all he had acquired in his fleshly pursuits were emptiness and disillusionment. One important lesson King Solomon learned was that living a self-centered life of affluence, seeking worldly pleasures apart from God, was futile and did not result in true happiness.

True happiness occurs when we find our joy, peace, and fulfillment in God. King Solomon concluded that we should reverence God and give His Word first place in our lives—for this is the whole duty of man. If we try to meet our own needs, we will be doing it in our own energy and strength, which will bring us unnecessary stress, difficulty, and spiritual warfare. As Christians, we must heed the words of Ephesians 6:11: "Put on the full armor of God so that you can take your stand against the devil's schemes."

When God gives us what we need, His supernatural grace is in full operation. On the other hand, when we do not obey Matthew 6:33, then we'll worry about how we are going to manage to get all of our needs met.

Frequently, the cares of the world creep in to choke out the Word of God and His joy in our lives. Because the world is opposed to Jesus Christ and His people, it will always resist the principles of His kingdom. Today's society pressures us to rather spend our time loving ourselves by working hard for more money to build our own successful dynasties.

In contrast, God's way involves investing in a heavenly bank account that will last forever; no rust or corruption can touch our eternal deposit. Whenever we have a need, we must activate our faith, asking our heavenly Father for what we need, and He will give it to us. First John 5:14 assures us, "This is the confidence we have in approaching God: that if we ask anything according to his will, he hears us."

God desires for us to agree with His way of thinking, rather than conforming to that of the world system. Isaiah 55:8 says, "For my thoughts are not your thoughts, neither are your ways my ways, declares the Lord." Our way of thinking needs to be renewed by the Word of God, thereby empowering us through the Holy Spirit to no longer conform to the world's philosophies.

Our covenant-keeping God desires for His children to receive the blessings of His covenant. As believers, we have a responsibility to do our part when we make a covenant with God. Unfortunately, we often fall short of doing our part by choosing to "do our own thing," ultimately breaking our covenant with

Him. The good news for us is that He will always be faithful to carry out His part. Numbers 23:19a says, "God is not a man, that he should lie, nor a son of man that he should change his mind." Since God's very nature involves faithfulness, He will always provide for our daily needs.

We do not manage our time well because we spend too many hours trying to provide for ourselves or seeking after worldly things. This robs us of time to do the work of the kingdom of God. Matthew 6:25-30 says it best when Jesus tells us not to worry about providing for the necessities of life such as what we are going to wear or eat. "If God takes care of the birds and the lilies of the field," Jesus said, "how much more will He take care of us who are more valuable to Him?" When we let God reign in our lives, then we can rest assured that He will take full responsibility for taking care of our needs. When I choose to believe that God will give me all that I need for my daily provision, I don't worry; I simply activate my faith.

Sometimes we make things too complicated. If we take God at His Word and make it the final authority in our lives, then we will become radically transformed into the very image of Christ. By displaying the nature of Christ, we will be able to do great things according to His Word. When we exercise our faith, God will allow His grace to abound toward us by giving us all that we need as He wills (2 Corinthians 9:8). The primary things for us to do are putting God first and believing that God will be faithful to do what He said He would do.

Some may say, "I still need to do something to live and plan for the future." The Lord is not telling us to refrain from *planning* for tomorrow. Planning for the future can be time well spent when we seek God's counsel first; but *worrying* about tomorrow is time wasted. The negative by-products of worry and anxiety negate our faith and trust in God, disconnecting us from a stress-free and prosperous life, as well as causing damage to our physical health through stress.

As I meditated on this biblical principle of sowing and reaping, it made perfect sense to me. When I sow my time in God's kingdom, I will reap a harvest of blessings from His kingdom. Since that's the case, why would the believer *not* obey Matthew 6:33?

During my quiet time one day, I asked the Lord this question, and He revealed to me that it was an issue of trust. The bottom line is, can we trust God with our lives? While thinking about that question, I realized that sometimes I do not trust God with the affairs of my life. I should always trust Him because He loves me so much that He gave His Son Jesus to die for my sins. Looking back over my life, I recognized that God has never failed me, but I have often failed Him. I then asked God to forgive me for not trusting Him. The Lord is so gracious and longsuffering with us, but He still wants us to trust Him.

Trust can be defined as holding a firm belief in another's honesty, ability, or integrity. It means you believe that person will do exactly what he says he will do—no matter what. Many believers may think that they trust God because they obey Him, but trusting God really comes down to whether we believe what He says is true or not. That settles it right there for me: I choose to believe God and His Word according to what the Scriptures say. God cannot lie; His word is trustworthy and will endure forever. Psalms 9:10 says, "Those who know your name will trust in you, for you, Lord, have never forsaken those who seek you."

When we seek God's kingdom and His righteousness as we are asked to do in Matthew 6:33, God will never forsake us; He will meet all our needs according to His will. Our responsibility is to trust Him. If we do not trust Him, then we will vainly use our time to take care of all those things that have already have been provided for us. Many of us will become frustrated and dissatisfied with our lives because we are living beneath our royal privileges by seeking after the servant's portion instead of the royal portion.

Because we are members of the kingdom of God, a royal priesthood, and joint-heirs with Christ our King who owns everything, God wants to take care of us. The Lord reminded me that until we take the time to really get to know

Him, we will not entrust Him with our time to do what He created us to do. This insight on trusting God with my life has motivated me to learn more about His Word and spend more time getting to know God better. How much time do we spend getting to know someone that we think we can trust, only to find out that we really cannot trust them? People can fail us, but God cannot fail us.

Now I can understand why people may not do what is required of them in Matthew 6:33 so God will provide for all their needs. If they do not trust God, then it would drive them to work harder to provide for the things that they need. As believers, we must renew our minds with the Word of God so that its authority will occupy the first place in our lives. Then, when the issue of trust comes up concerning the faithfulness of God, it will be easy to understand Proverbs 3:5-6: "Trust in the Lord with all your heart and lean not on your own understanding; in all your ways acknowledge him, and he will make your paths straight." When we allow God's Word to have the final authority in our lives, then we do not need to figure out every minor detail of a situation.

Sometimes we pursue the wrong things, which costs us time. Colossians 3:1-2 says that we are to seek those things that are above, where Christ sits at the right hand of God. The "things that are above" are eternal and spiritual: God's word, His kingdom, His righteousness, His peace, and His joy. We need to esteem these spiritual things above all other things so we can enter into a place to enjoy them.

Seeking His righteousness means living according to His kingdom standards of right and wrong in relationship to both God and man. The Lord showed me that we often experience difficulty gaining a clear vision of how to seek the kingdom of God and His righteousness. To give us a better understanding of this principle, the next chapters will explain what the kingdom of God and His righteousness are.

Chapter 3

WHAT IS
THE KINGDOM OF GOD?

To understand how to seek the kingdom of God, it is necessary to define what the kingdom is. Webster's Dictionary defines "kingdom" as the "eternal, spiritual sovereignty of God or Christ; the realm of this sovereignty; and a realm or sphere in which one thing is dominant." The "kingdom" mentioned in Matthew 6:33 comes from the Greek word *basileia*, denoting royalty, rule, sovereignty, and dominion. Derived from the words "king" and "domain," a kingdom is the realm over which the king rules completely.

Jesus is King of kings and Lord of lords, and *He* is the one who is dominant in His kingdom. John 1:3 says, "All things were made by him; and without him was not any thing made that was made" (KJV). God created all things in heaven and in the earth—visible and invisible (Colossians 1:16). The kingdom of God involves the invisible realm of the spirit ruling over the visible realm of man. In other words, God is king over *everything*.

The nature of God's kingdom is eternal, spiritual, and full of light. The kingdom also asserts itself with divine power over Satan's rule and dominion. It is governed by the righteousness of Christ, which provides a holy standard for living godly lives.

Let's take a closer look at the eternal aspects of the kingdom of God. Jeremiah 10:10 says, "But the Lord is the true God, he is the living God, and an everlasting king . . ." (KJV). God Himself is eternal, and even the apostle Paul praises Him as the "King eternal, immortal, invisible, the only wise God" (1 Timothy 1:17, KJV). God's "dominion is an everlasting dominion, and His kingdom is from generation to generation" (Daniel 4:34, KJV).

God has prepared His kingdom for His people since the creation of the world (Matthew 25:34). The Lord desires for us to focus on His kingdom because we have a tendency to center all our attention instead on the things in the world. The Lord desires for us to be blessed in the natural as well as in the spiritual because He created us to live in both realms. He also knew, however, that if we did not seek Him first, those things in the natural would completely occupy our minds and hearts.

Unlike the temporal things of this world, God's kingdom is eternal. Second Corinthians 4:18 says that we should fix our eyes on what is unseen instead of what is seen; for what is seen is temporal or temporary, but what is unseen is eternal. Temporal things are subject to change, but eternal things are not. Likewise, God and His Word are eternal. He desires for us to take dominion over the things of the world by using our faith, which is "the substance of things hoped for, the evidence of things not seen" (Hebrew 11:1, KJV).

The Lord desires for us to seek His kingdom, expecting to bring what is spiritual into the natural by faith so that we can glorify Him. The kingdom of God has eternal values that are governed by His Word, which are spirit and life. When we seek His kingdom, we are seeking both Him and His Word because they are one and the same.

Colossians 3:1-2 says, "Since, then, you have been raised with Christ, set your hearts on things above, where Christ is seated at the right hand of God. Set your minds on things above, not on earthly things." God's priority for us is to focus on Him and strive to put His priorities into daily practice. Since we are born again, we put on the new man who desires spiritual things that are eternal (Colossians 3:10). When we seek the Lord first, He will help us to strike a balance between the acquisition of spiritual things as well as natural things. The Lord knows, for example, that we need to eat and have clothes and other necessities of life. Just as He takes care of the birds of the air and the lilies of the field, He will do much more for us because He loves us. In addition to our physical needs, the Lord knows that we need spiritual things as well because our spirit is housed in a body that possesses a soul. In both the natural and spiritual realms, He has called us to live by faith.

First John 5:4 states, "For whatsoever is born of God overcometh the world: and this is the victory that overcometh the world, even our faith" (KJV). Our spiritual man needs spiritual things like faith; the Word of God, which is spirit and life; righteousness, which allows us to be in right standing with God; and so much more that we learn about by studying the Word of God.

We need to re-evaluate how we manage our time. Are we using our time to seek after worldly things that are here today and gone tomorrow more than we are seeking the kingdom of God? Jesus makes it clear that we are not to store up for ourselves treasures on earth, where moth and rust can destroy them or thieves can steal them (Matthew 6:19). It is better for us rather to invest our time in eternal things that are above because they are not subject to change or corruption. Some of our eternal blessings include Christ Jesus, who is our Lord and Savior and our High Priest; our righteousness, which is found in Christ who is seated in heavenly places, far above principalities and rulers of darkness; and eternal life in Christ, which is our eternal security.

Our spiritual position is above the natural because we are raised up together with Christ and seated in the heavenly places in Christ Jesus (Ephesians 2:6). What we focus on is what we have. If we concentrate our attention on eternal things, then we will obtain eternal things. On the other hand, if we focus on earthly things, we will receive earthly things and put ourselves on the same level as those things. When we fix our eyes on the kingdom, then we'll become kingdom-minded and acquire those things that belong to the King who owns everything.

God's kingdom is not only eternal, but it is also spiritual. In Luke 17: 20-21, Jesus was asked by the Pharisees when the kingdom of God would come. Jesus replied that it would not come with observation, because the kingdom of God "is within you." The present nature of the kingdom is spiritual and within the hearts of born-again believers. The Pharisees were expecting the kingdom of God to come down as an earthly, political power. They did not know that they were talking to the King, whose kingdom had already come (Luke 1:30-33). During His three-year ministry, Jesus frequently shared this message: "Repent: for the kingdom of heaven is at hand" (Matthew 4:17, KJV).

When the King came to earth as a man, the kingdom followed Him wherever He went, defeating the enemies of God; sickness and demonic oppression were not welcome in Jesus' presence. The true kingdom is spiritual—inward rather than outward—and begins with the work of the Holy Spirit in the lives of His people. In John 3:3-5, Jesus tells Nicodemus that except a man be born again, he cannot see the kingdom of God. He continued in verse 6, "That which is born of the flesh is flesh and that which is born of the Spirit is spirit." Jesus told the woman at the well that "God is a Spirit: and they that worship him must worship him in spirit and in truth (John 4:24, KJV). In John 14:6, Jesus says that He is the way, the truth, and the life. Thus, in order for us to worship God in spirit and truth, we must be united with Christ, who is truth, and come to God with a sincere heart directed by the Holy Spirit, who will reveal the truth of the Father that is revealed in the Son.

The word "truth" comes from the Greek word *aletheia*, which is the primary characteristic of God. After the Spirit of God comes to live within our hearts, He can communicate to our spirits those things pertaining to God's kingdom. In order to worship the King, we must worship Him in spirit and truth. The Holy Spirit is the Spirit of truth; He will guide us into all truth and show us things to come. In order for us to worship God in spirit and truth, we need to allow our spirit to be led by the Spirit of God.

As believers, we need to remember that we are in the world but not *of* the world, which seeks after pleasure. We can easily get entangled with the things of the world and begin seeking after those things that are temporal, instead of those that are eternal. When that happens, we will live like those people in the world who are wasting their time trying to please themselves by accumulating things that are likely to decay. On the other hand, when we choose to focus our attention on eternal things such as God's Word, as well as righteousness, peace, and joy in the Holy Spirit, it will enable us to live a kingdom life.

God's kingdom is not only eternal and spiritual, but it is also one of light. "God is light; in him there is no darkness at all (1 John 1:5)." God dwells in a realm of unapproachable light that is totally different and far above His creation. Yet, He calls us out of darkness into His marvelous light. Those who accept this call declare praises unto Him for our salvation (1 Peter 1:8- 9). Moreover, God desires for us to share in the inheritance of the saints in the kingdom of light (Colossians 1:12). God's light has come into the world through His Son Jesus, but people loved darkness because their deeds were evil. Everyone who does evil hates the light and will not come into the light because they fear that their deeds will be exposed (John 3:19-20).

God has given each person the free will to choose to exchange the dominion of darkness—a metaphor for sin—for the dominion of light. The effects of sin include sickness, death, misery, and ignorance to the truth of His Word. It is up to us to cast aside the deeds of darkness and put on the armor of light by submitting to God, who is Light, and walking in Love, who is God. That is why it is very important to seek the kingdom of God (which is also the kingdom of light), because the things of this world will cause us to gratify the desires of the sinful nature.

First John 1:6-7 says, "If we claim to have fellowship with him yet walk in the darkness, we lie and do not live by the truth. But if we walk in the light, as he is in the light, we have fellowship with one another, and the blood of Jesus, his Son, purifies us from all sin." We have a responsibility to walk in the light. When we do walk in the light of God's Word, it will not only reveal but also remove any areas of darkness in our lives.

If we sin against God, His Word says, "If we confess our sins, he is faithful and just and will forgive us our sins, and purify us from all unrighteousness" (1 John 1:9).

The Lord does not want us to continue indulging in a lifestyle of sin. The sinful nature (the flesh) wars against our spirit, striving to fulfill the lustful desires that it so desperately craves. Romans 7:18 states that there is no good thing that dwells in the flesh; therefore, we should not make any provisions for the flesh (Romans 13:14). Many times we feed our flesh with immoral things such as TV programs that portray sexual impurity, movies that blatantly show pornographic and adulterous scenes, and music that promotes sexual pleasures. All of these things and more feed the flesh and appeal to the lust of the eyes. First John 2:16 says, "For all that is in the world, the lust of the flesh, and the lust of the eyes, and the pride of life, is not of the Father, but is of the world."

Even the subtle things, such as buying and accumulating clothes and other things when we don't need to buy them, involve the lust of the flesh. The pride of life is grossly evident when we boast about what we have acquired or how much success we have achieved in life. These fleshly desires compete with our spiritual desires for control of our lives. We even see this in the lack of self-control with our appetite for food, resulting in overeating.

When we are not disciplined in seeking after the kingdom of God and His righteousness, then we will keep on struggling. We can use our time in a more productive way by studying the Word of God, which clearly defines the righteous and godly standards pertaining to how we should govern ourselves according to kingdom values.

Romans 8:5 says, "Those who live according to the sinful nature have their minds set on what that nature desires; but those who live in accordance with the Spirit have their minds set on what the Spirit desires." We have to count ourselves dead to sin and alive to Christ, using self-discipline to put our bodies under subjection to the king's rule. When we seek after God's kingdom values and submit ourselves to the authority of God's Word, we will be able to resist those temptations when they arise.

Some believers ask why they are still tempted, since they have been born again by the Spirit. Just because we become Christians, however, does not mean that Satan's temptations will stop. Yet, we can resist the temptation to sin against God by turning to Him to strengthen us in our time of weakness. When we are weak, God is strong. Even though temptation is an invitation to sin, we don't have to succumb to it. To help us resist it, we will need a power much higher than our own—the power of God. Remember, temptation is not from God, but it comes from evil desires that are placed within our hearts as bait from the enemy to lure us out from under the protective shadow of the Almighty and into the snare of sin.

This is why it is important to continue to walk in the light and not in the darkness. As members of God's kingdom of light, we are given the privilege of letting our lights shine in a dark and corrupt world. God desires for us to enjoy the things that He created for us, but we must first submit ourselves to His lordship, His Word, and His Spirit, which will empower us to live a self-disciplined kingdom life. For once we were in darkness, but now we are living in the light of the Lord. We need to live as children of light (Ephesians 5:8).

God's kingdom is spiritual, eternal, and full of light, but it also comes with His almighty power. According to 1 Corinthians 4:20, God's kingdom is not a "matter of talk but of power." The kingdom of God reveals itself in power and triumphs over Satan's rule and dominion. This overcoming power flows from the Holy Spirit, who empowers the believer to conquer the powers of Satan and his demonic influences. According to 1 John 3:8, the Son of God was manifested to destroy the works of the devil. Christ came in power to rescue souls from the kingdom of darkness and transport them into His kingdom of light.

The word "power" comes from the Greek word *dunamis*, which means absolute strength and might or power in action. The heavenly kingdom primarily is a demonstration of His divine power in action. In Acts 26:18, Jesus commissioned Saul (later known as the apostle Paul) to preach the gospel regarding His power that was available to free all those enslaved by Satan in the kingdom of darkness. As believers, it is important for us to understand that the greater one lives inside of us; His power is greater than Satan's, which is operating in the world, outside of us (1 John 4:4).

Dunamis, which describes the power of God, is the word from which "dynamite" is derived. I think of the power of God as the dynamite used to blow up Satan's kingdom. We must remember that when we seek the kingdom of God, we have full access to His power to use against Satan's kingdom and his demonic influences. In Mark 16:17, Jesus promised His disciples that He would supply them with this mighty power to "drive out demons . . . pick up snakes with their hands . . . [and] place their hands on sick people, and they will get well."

Satan will use the things of the world, our evil desires, and our weaknesses in his attempt to destroy our marriages with separation, divorce, financial ruin, adultery, and much more. We have to take the time to guard what we receive into our eye gates and ear gates. We often see or hear sinful things in the TV shows, movies, videos, and music of our culture that plant harmful seeds in our memory bank for Satan to use later to trigger evil thoughts in our minds.

Words have the power to create pictures—for good or evil. As believers, we have the Greater One living within our spirits to empower us to take captive every thought and make it obedient to Christ (2 Corinthians 10:3-5). We do not have to allow our thoughts to be ruled by worldly corruption that has a negative influence on what we think or do. Although we possess God's power to cast down those thoughts, do we really want to waste precious time casting down evil thoughts because we did not use self-discipline to protect our eye or ear gates from what we watched or listened to?

When we manage our time God's way, we need to keep our focus on God's kingdom values. The world will say that it is all right to watch those movies or soap operas that promote perverted and explicit sex, adulterous relationships, and other immoral acts. Many of us are not aware of Satan's strategy to desensitize their moral values through the media. We need to remember, however, that what we focus on is what we'll have.

When God opened my eyes to the futile way I was managing my time, it made more sense to me to invest in His kingdom. The majority of my time was used to go to work and church, but I did not seek God's counsel on what I should do with the rest of my time. God told me that I was not doing what He created me to do, so to Him, I was doing nothing, which was slothful. I began to take time to read and study the Bible to learn about God's principles for living a kingdom life without stress. My study on the subjects also has helped me to know who I am in Christ and that I can do all things through Him.

I began to watch less TV. When I did, I watched programs on the Christian networks or shows that had decent content. I also checked to see what my daughters were watching or listening to: many times, parents do not take the time to find out, only to discover too late that their children are exposed to ungodly words and visual images.

God's power is available to turn us away from the kingdom of darkness and bring us into the kingdom of light. The moral decay of our world today, especially in the school system and with family values, should get the attention of all believers to re-evaluate how they are managing their time.

More parents, for example, should take time to teach their children godly moral values. How many parents know the Bible? How many of us pray with and for our children during the day? Do we get involved in their school activities or their work, or do we just let them take care of themselves? Sometimes it means just spending fifteen minutes with them or having a meal together. On the other hand, when we allow the TV or the world to influence our children, we could pay a high price with our time, money, and peace later to get them out of trouble, jail, or some other life-threatening situation. We have to stop and ask ourselves, what is important to the Lord—the world's values or His values?

We also can ask ourselves how much time we lost doing it our way instead of God's way.

Even for those of us who are managing our time God's way, we should be more involved in sharing the gospel, as well as being living epistles, so that the unbelievers can have the opportunity to receive the good news about Christ dying on the cross for their sins and believe in His finished work. Then, they can be saved and rescued from Satan's dominion of darkness and come into God's kingdom. Romans 1:16 says that we are not ashamed of the gospel because it is the *power* of God for the salvation of everyone who believes.

We also need to use our time to help other believers get free from the demonic powers of oppression that try to keep them in bondage. It will take the efforts of those who are strong in the Lord to help those who are too weak to stand against the wiles of the devil. This is another reason God wants us to keep our focus on things above and not on things in the world: to empower us to help others who are struggling.

According to Ephesians 2:6, we were raised up together with Christ to be seated in the heavenly realms. When we seek the kingdom of God with all of its power, we are keeping our focus on Christ Jesus, who is seated at the right hand of God. Ephesians 1:20 tells us that God's great power raised Him from the dead, far above the rulers of darkness and Satan's demonic hierarchy. God wants us to pay close attention to the truth concerning our spiritual position in Christ. If Christ is far above Satan's demonic hierarchy and we are raised in Him, then our spiritual position in Christ is also above Satan's domain.

This is why we need to keep our focus on God's kingdom and on those things above. Colossians 3:2-3 reminds us to set our minds on things above, not on earthly things, because God wants us to see things from His perspective, which is far beyond circumstances, trials, tribulations, and a limited scope for our future. We have access to His Word, His power, His grace, and His blessings. Why would we not seek His kingdom first?

One day, I was meditating on Ephesians 3:20, which states that "God is able to do immeasurably more than all we ask or imagine, according to his power that is at work within us." God told me that He was looking for a remnant of people who would push past the natural realm and begin to see from His perspective what they could only dare to imagine right now. This prompted me to develop my perception of the deep things that concerned God and then come into agreement with Him for them to come to pass. This Scripture passage is conditional, depending on the Holy Spirit's presence, power, and grace operating in our lives. For that kind of power to flow, we need to invest our time in seeking both the kingdom of God and His righteousness. God is always willing to bring the increase in our lives. This is the reason why the apostle Paul prayed for the Ephesians to have this incomparable great power working with them and through them (Ephesians 1:19). It is the same resurrection power that raised Jesus from the dead and now resides in every believer.

As previously stated, God created us to live in two realms: the spiritual and the physical. We operate in the spiritual realm by living and abiding in Christ, but we live abundantly in the natural realm by allowing Christ's redemptive rule to direct our lives. Ephesians 3:14-19 shows us that God desires us to be strengthened with power through His Spirit in our inner being so that Christ may establish His presence in our hearts that we may be rooted and established in His love, so that we may comprehend and experience Christ's love in our lives, and that we may be filled with the fullness of God. That is powerful: why would we not invest our time in God's kingdom when there is so much to gain by allowing Christ to rule in our hearts and submitting to the leading and guidance of the Holy Spirit? When we submit to God's kingdom principles, we will reflect the characteristics of our Lord Jesus Christ from our innermost being.

Acts 1:8 says that we believers will receive power when the Holy Spirit comes on us. God not only desires for each person to be born again, but also to receive His power through the baptism of the Holy Spirit. As His witnesses, we will not do business as usual when we receive this *dunamis* power. It means more than mere strength or ability: it is power demonstrated in operation. When the power of the Holy Spirit is operating, we can drive out evil spirits, heal the sick, and deliver the oppressed and depressed from satanic oppression by the authority of Jesus. The Spirit will also empower us to be effective witnesses when we share the gospel, which is the power of God for everyone that believes in Christ Jesus.

God wants all people to be saved and born again by His Spirit to become a part of the kingdom of God. The basic requirement is to repent and be born again of the Spirit of God (John 3:3). God is waiting for each person, as an act of his will, to "repent." The word "repent" comes from the Greek word *mentano*, meaning "to turn around." It involves turning away from evil ways, then turning to Christ and through Christ to God. No one comes to God the Father unless they come through Christ Jesus (John 14:6). God's power is available to rescue sinners from Satan's dominion, but it is up to them to choose to put their faith in Christ Jesus and surrender their ways to God's way. Then, the Holy Spirit will empower them to live kingdom lives.

Now that we have a grasp of the concept of the kingdom of God, we can take time to understand His righteousness as well. Romans 14:17 says, "For the kingdom of God is not meat and drink; but righteousness, and peace, and joy in the Holy Ghost (KJV)." These aspects are spiritual, and we can experience them in our hearts where God's kingdom is ruling. Because His kingdom is governed by His righteous standards, we need to know what His righteousness is in order to live in subjection to His rule.

Chapter 4

SEEKING GOD'S RIGHTEOUSNESS

The Holy Spirit empowers believers to live a righteous life, be at peace with God and man, and experience the joy of the Lord. Our time on this earth should be used to seek after both the kingdom of God and His righteousness.

The word "righteousness" is derived from the Greek word *dikaiosune*, which means "purity of heart and rectitude of life, or being and doing right." The righteousness of God involves divine holiness applied to the moral conduct that governs God's people. Romans 3:22 says, "This righteousness from God comes through faith in Jesus Christ to all who believe." Paul goes on to say in chapter 12:3 that "God has given to every man a measure of faith." The writer of Hebrews affirms, "Now faith is the substance of things hoped for, the evidence of things not seen (Hebrews 11:1, KJV). When we put our faith in Jesus Christ, we are firmly believing and trusting in the crucified and risen Christ as our personal Lord and Savior.

Second Corinthians 5:21 says that "God made him who had no sin to be sin for us, so that in him we might become the righteousness of God." The perfect righteousness of Christ is imputed to the believer when he accepts Christ as his Savior. Now, the believer is not under condemnation because the life of Christ and His righteousness have set him free from the law of sin and death (Romans 8:1-2). The apostle Paul realized this was true when he considered all that he gained loss when compared to the greatness of knowing Christ as his Lord and Savior (Philippians 3:7). The righteous requirements of the law are fully met in those who do not live in accordance to the sinful nature, but according to the Spirit.

It is important to understand why we must make it a priority to seek the righteousness of God. If we do not, then the sinful nature will be fixed on what it desires. Those who live according to the Spirit, however, will have their minds set on what the Spirit desires. The good news is that God does not call us to live righteously without first giving us a way to do it: He gave His Son, Jesus Christ, "who bore our sins in His body on the cross so that we might die to sins and live for righteousness" (1 Peter 2: 24).

As believers, we have the power of the Holy Spirit working in our lives to overcome sin. It is our responsibility to live our lives according to the direction of the Spirit of God. Of course, there is a conflict with the sinful nature and the Spirit; the sinful nature desires to take pleasure in and be occupied with gratifying its corrupt desires. Galatians 5:19-21 says, "The acts of the sinful nature are obvious: sexual immorality, impurity and debauchery; idolatry and witchcraft; hatred, discord, jealousy, fits of rage, selfish ambition, dissensions, factions and envy; drunkenness, orgies, and the like. I warn you, as I did before, that those who live like this will not inherit the kingdom of God." If we do not make it a priority to seek the righteousness of God, then the sinful nature will strive to take control.

God helped me understand this concept by giving me the analogy of two sets of antennas. One set was for my spirit man, which desires to be led by the Spirit of God, and the other set was for the sinful nature (my flesh), which opposes God. God reminded me that if I feed my spirit the food of the kingdom, it will be more sensitive and tuned to receive more guidance and empowerment from the Spirit. This helps my spirit man to become more sensitive to His voice, His presence, and His prodding. If I feed my flesh with things that are contrary to the will of God, it will be more sensitive to moral corruption and sin, thus hindering me from submitting to God. The more I feed my spirit, the more my spiritual antennas will be attuned to receive from the Holy Spirit. When I make no provision for the flesh, the sinful nature's antennas are too weak and disabled to take in the corruption of the world.

I learned a valuable lesson from this illustration. If I allow my spirit to be fed spiritual food from the Word of God that instructs me and gives me spiritual guidance, then my spirit will be controlled and led by the Holy Spirit to help me live a holy and righteous life. This is why we need to invest our time in seeking God's righteousness—so that we can be empowered to live in communion with the Spirit of Christ. Those who practice a lifestyle that yields to the acts of the sinful nature cannot inherit God's kingdom (Galatians 5:21). We must rather yield to the spontaneous work of the Holy Spirit to develop and cultivate the fruit of the Spirit in us, which are the by-products of living for God.

The fruit of the Spirit is love, joy, peace, longsuffering, gentleness, goodness, faith, meekness, and temperance (Galatians 5:22-23). There is a clear contrast between the lifestyle of the Spirit-filled believer and that of a person controlled by his sinful nature. As believers, we cannot afford to entertain thoughts of engaging in acts of the sinful nature. It is vital that we protect our eye gates and ear gates, because what we take in can have influence over what we do. We must remember that Satan uses our sinful desires and the things of the world to tempt us to sin against God. It is the responsibility of the believer to keep a single-minded focus on kingdom living. As believers, we have too much at stake if we want to inherit the kingdom of God. We must therefore resist sin and "put to death the misdeeds of the body (Romans 8:13)."

The struggle for believers is whether we will give in to the sinful nature and succumb to sin or yield to the Spirit's leading and guidance. Satan is working overtime to get us to yield to the sinful nature so that we will put ourselves back under the law to be overwhelmed by condemnation and guilt. The apostle Paul reassures us, however, with these words: "Therefore, there is now no condemnation for those who are in Christ Jesus, because through Christ Jesus the law of the Spirit of life set me free from the law of sin and death. For what the law was powerless to do in that it was weakened by the sinful nature, God did by sending his own Son in the likeness of sinful man to be a sin offering" (Romans 8:1-3).

I spend more time in fellowship with God and His Word now because that helps me to live a righteous and holy life through the power of the Holy Spirit. When we seek God's righteousness, we submit to the Holy Spirit's direction and enabling power to help us do what we cannot do in our own strength. We believers need self-discipline to keep us from seeking after those things that satisfy the sinful nature.

The Bible is full of God's holy instructions to help us renew our minds. We need to have our minds conformed to God's way of thinking and His way of living. Without holiness, those who are controlled by the sinful nature cannot please God. It is in our best interest to seek after God's righteousness.

Matthew 5:6 says, "Blessed are those who hunger and thirst after righteousness for they will be filled." Hunger and thirst need to be satisfied in order to live; we don't need to waste our time trying to gratify them with the things of the world that can only offer a temporary satisfaction. When we truly desire righteousness to satisfy our spiritual appetite, then we will be fully satisfied as God quenches our thirst and satisfies our hunger with more of Himself. Psalms 42:1 reminds us that our soul should thirst for God just as the deer thirsts for water. Just as our lives are dependent on water, so should our lives be dependent on the righteousness of God.

One day during my quiet time with God, He shared with me a concern for His people's appetites, which were being filled with ungodly, worldly things. Sometimes, believers cannot see any evidence of righteousness in their own lives because of a lack of self-discipline and a stubborn refusal to yield to the Holy Spirit's demands.

Many Christians become so carnal-minded that they cannot be distinguished from the people in the world. In 1 Corinthians 3:1-3, the apostle Paul admonished the believers in Corinth about the very same situation, pointing out the evidence of carnality—envying, strife, and divisions—among them. Some of them were behaving in a worldly manner instead of consistently resisting the desires of their sinful nature. They were acting like baby Christians or new converts who did not yet understand the full impact of their newfound salvation in Christ. Paul also warns the believers in Galatia not to let their flesh control them, encouraging them to live by the Spirit instead (Galatians 5:16).

We have the grace of God and the Holy Spirit to help us live according to God's righteous standards. This grace is extended to all who will receive it. Some sinners may believe that they are "good" people, and certainly God knows about their supposed "goodness" that can only be viewed through the glasses of their own self-righteous standards. According to Isaiah 64:6, however, all of our righteous acts are like filthy rags. We can waste our time seeking after what the world values as good, only to find out when we stand before God on Judgment Day that we were full of self-righteous pride—not the righteousness provided by Christ's death on the cross that allows us to come into His presence.

God's righteousness is expressed by believers remaining in Christ (John 15:4). God is making a demand on what He has already given. Once we accept Christ as our personal Savior and Lord, then we'll receive eternal life and the power of His Spirit to remain in Him. As long as we abide in Christ, His life, along with His righteousness, will continue to flow through us. We must make it a priority to seek God's righteousness in order to thrive in His kingdom. Jesus is ruling in the hearts of His people and His kingdom with a scepter of righteousness (Hebrews 1:8).

As the Prince of Peace, Jesus not only upholds His kingdom with justice and righteousness, but also with peace. Jesus gave us His peace, which is not like that of the world (John 14:27), so that we can be joined to Him. The word "peace" in this scriptural passage comes from the Greek word *eirene*, meaning "to join." Whenever there is peace between two parties, it results in a joining.

On the other hand, whenever there is strife or enmity between two parties, it causes a separation. When Jesus Christ paid the price for our sins with His blood, He made atonement for our sins. Jesus' *at-one-ment* reconciled man back to God, making the way for God and man to be *at one* again (Romans 5:1).

Because peace brings unity, there is a continuous tug-of-war between the world which wants us to be joined to its way, and God who wants us to be joined to His holiness and righteousness. If we choose to be joined with God, then we are distinctly separated from the world. This ongoing struggle leads us to ask the question: "Will we be at peace with God or with the world?" In Ephesians 2:14-16, we see that Christ Jesus is our peace; He made the two one by destroying the dividing wall of hostility. Through His death on the cross, Christ made it possible for all people to be reconciled to God. God's peace is available to join us to Him, but we must choose to yield our way to His way.

When we surrender our lives to Jesus, the God of peace will sanctify us through every part of our being: our spirit, soul, and our body (1 Thessalonians 5:23). Moreover, God wants us to make every effort to live in peace with all men and to be holy; without holiness none of us will see the Lord (Hebrews 12:14).

Peace stands like an umpire to guard over our hearts, allowing us to remain stable throughout all our emotional trials. God will allow this particular fruit of the Spirit to be cultivated and nurtured in the midst of a storm so that He can manifest His peace through our lives.

Now, we can rejoice in the Lord, secure in knowing that we have the righteousness of God to live according to the kingdom's moral standards, along with the peace of God that transcends all understanding. The more we know about God, the more we will understand why His peace separates us from sin, worldly desires, and ungodly people and then joins us to His righteousness and holiness.

Another expression of the kingdom of God is joy, also a fruit of the Spirit. The word "joy" comes from the Greek word *chara*, which means quietness of heart and mind based on the knowledge of the love, peace, and grace of God. Joy also springs forth from the revelation knowledge of who God is and how near He is to us when we are going through some difficult times. In Hebrews 13:5, God promises that He will never leave us nor forsake us.

The third chapter of Daniel portrays how the Lord was with Shadrach, Meshach, and Abednego when they were thrown into the fiery furnace. They rejoiced despite their persecution, knowing that their God was more than able to save them, but if He chose not to, they would continue to put their faith and trust in Him.

This kind of joy is based on our reconciliation with God and the reassuring presence of the Spirit of God that follows it. The apostle Paul offers this blessing to the church in Rome: "May the God of hope fill you with all joy and peace as you trust in Him, so that you may overflow with hope by the power of the Holy Spirit" (Romans 15:13). We need the joy of the Lord, which gives us strength to fight the good fight of faith and helps us press beyond those hard times that would try to keep us discouraged.

Joy is the easiest fruit of the Spirit to lose. When life's problems come our way, Satan will try to steal our joy by making us feel sad and depressed. This is why Philippians 4:4 says to rejoice always in the Lord. Even when we don't feel like rejoicing, we should come into agreement with God to rejoice so that this fruit can be cultivated and work for our good. James 1:2 says to "consider it pure joy" whenever we face trials and situations in life.

Joy is not the same as happiness. Happiness comes from the word "happen;" therefore, happiness is based on what is happening in our lives. The joy of the Lord allows us to walk through the storms of life, knowing that He will be with us, no matter how bad it looks on the surface. We can see how this worked for Christ Jesus by the joy that was set before Him to endure the cross (Hebrews 12:2). God will give us joy to overcome the trials and tribulations in our lives so we can endure to cross the finish lines of our individual races.

God has given us His "righteousness, peace, and joy in the Holy Ghost" to enable us to live a kingdom lifestyle. It will cost us our valuable time to allow the Holy Spirit to show us how to submit every aspect of our lives to God. I will discuss some spiritual disciplines in Chapter 9 that have helped me to become more disciplined in my faith walk.

God has our best interests at heart. He knows that we need to seek both His kingdom and His righteousness in order for us to experience a prosperous and stress-free life. Now that we understand more about what His kingdom and righteousness is, we will be able to seek God first instead of our way or the world's way. The Lord desires for us to gain a clear vision of where He is taking us through this life journey. It is our responsibility to acquire knowledge and understanding of what is important to God. The Lord placed on my heart that what we need to do the most is spend time with Him, getting to know Him.

How many of us take the time to get to know God? Do we read and study the Bible to learn what it says about His attributes, His character, and His relationships to His people? Do we really know the One who created all things and knows all things, even at the time when we will depart this earth?

Chapter 5

SEEKING TO KNOW GOD

It is important for us to really know God in order for us to seek after His kingdom and His righteousness. We must not only know *of* Him but truly *know* Him in a personal way. Believers will always struggle with the principle of seeking the kingdom of God and His righteousness if they do not fully commit their lives to God and His will for their lives.

Matthew 6:33 requires us to fully commit our lives to God according to kingdom values, and then He will take care of our needs. In order for me to believe that someone will take care of my needs, I need to know the character of that person. I may ask some questions such as these: Is the person trustworthy? Does the person have my best interests at heart? Is the person reliable and dependable? Can he back up what he says?

How many of us spend too much of our time getting to know someone who tells us that he or she has our best interests at heart, only to find out that person actually does not, so we really did not know him or her after all? Did we take the time to know that person's character before we got involved in the relationship? Likewise, we need to know God's character so that we can fully commit ourselves to His lordship.

A good way to find out about God's character is by reading what the Word says about Him. The first thing we need to learn is that God is love, and He unselfishly loves everyone. We have to be fully persuaded that God loves us and has our best interests at heart. First John 4:7-8 says, "Dear friends, let us love one another, for love comes from God. Everyone who loves has been born of God and knows God. Whoever does not love does not know God, because God is love." When we are born of God, then God is in us. Since God is love, therefore, we also have love because God lives inside us. For us to know God, then, we have to be born of God.

There are many people who say that they know God, but actually they do not because they are not born of God. Once we are born again, then God pours out His love into our hearts by the Holy Spirit whom He has given to us (Romans 5:5). The word "love" comes from *agape*, a Greek word defining the very nature of God. *Agape* expresses the deep love and interest of a perfect God toward mankind which is unworthy in their sinful state. God hates sin, but He still loves us. The unbeliever cannot experience God's kind of love until he repents and places his faith in Christ Jesus; then he can experience the love of God in his heart.

God's love and the world's kind of love are not the same. The Standard Encyclopedic Dictionary defines love as "a deep devotion or affection for another person or persons;" an example of this is a love for one's children. Another definition of love is a strong sexual passion for another person, sexual passion in general, or the gratification of it.

The first definition of love pertains to parents who love their children regardless if they are doing unlovable things. One day while I was spending time with God, He told me to call my daughters to let them know that I love them no matter what they have done to upset me. I told them that I may be disappointed in what they did, but I would tell them the truth concerning their actions so they could expect consequences for their actions. Despite their misbehavior, I wanted to let them know that I would always love them.

My honest admission to my daughters really allowed me to see God the Father's great love for me as His child. Hebrews 12:6 says that God disciplines those He loves and He punishes everyone He accepts as a son. God's Word says that if our own earthly fathers disciplined us and we respected them for it, how much more should we submit to God the Father (Hebrews 12: 9)? God desires the very best for our lives, even when we don't understand why He disciplines us.

The difference between parents' love for their children and God's love for us, His people, is that God loved us unconditionally when He gave His Son to die for our sins. Real love is an action, not a feeling or emotion that is subject to what is going on around us. Real love or "agape" love will put the interests of others before our own. First John 3:16 says, "This is how we know what love is: Jesus Christ laid down his life for us. And we ought to lay down our lives for our brothers." God is not asking us to die for someone: Jesus Christ already paid the ultimate price for everyone. What this statement means is that we should serve others with no thought or motive of recovering anything in return. When we desire to know God, we also want to have *agape* love that looks out for the best interests of others. This truth concerning God's great love for mankind should further motivate us to pursue God as our first love.

No one can really love a person the way God desires him to until he first experiences God's love for himself. So many people are looking for love in the wrong places or for the wrong reasons because they are trying to fill a void —only to find out that God's love alone can satisfy that emptiness. It is only after they receive Christ as their Savior that they can pour out the love of God shed in their hearts into the lives of others.

Because the world system revolves around selfish satisfaction, it will always oppose this *agape*-type of love. If we believers will use the Word of God as our standard for defining love instead of allowing the world to impose its values on us, we will save a lot of time. Many of us would have been spared heartaches, painful disappointments, and a sense of loss from broken relationships if we had made it our top priority to spend time with our first love, God Himself.

Hence, we would have spent time learning what true love was all about and how to love someone according to what His Word says.

First Corinthians 13:4-7 defines love; love is God personified. This Scripture passage gives an apt description of this facet of God's character. Since God is love, I will interchange "God" for "love" in this scriptural passage: "God is patient, God is kind. God does not envy, God does not boast, God is not proud. God is not rude, God is not self-seeking, God is not easily angered, God keeps no record of wrongs. God does not delight in evil but rejoices with the truth. God always protects, always trusts, always hopes, always perseveres."

"Love never fails;" therefore, *God* never fails. God is love and love is God. If you do not have God living inside of you, then you do not have love. Anything apart from God is not love. Having God inside us is important because only then will we understand true love; any other type of love is simply an emotion. People are ruled by their emotions when they fall in love, most likely for the wrong reasons.

When we have God living within us, then we'll have true love living in us as well. We will be able to tell the difference between a person who has true love inside him from one who does not have true love when they say, "I love you." How many people have been deceived when certain individuals have showed them acts of kindness and said all the right things—only later to discover that they were not really sincere?

Many people are deceived by counterfeit love. Bank tellers who are being trained to identify counterfeit money only study the real money. Then, if any counterfeit bills show up, they can easily distinguish them from the real ones. That is the way it should be with God's love: we should seek after God as our first love, allowing Him to show us what true love is really like. Then, when counterfeit love comes our way, we can easily discern that it is not the real thing.

God does not want born-again believers to be unequally yoked with unbelievers who do not have this true love, because they will not know how to love us properly. We must heed 2 Corinthians 6:14, which says, "Do not be yoked together with unbelievers. For what do righteousness and wickedness have in common? Or what fellowship can light have with darkness?"

This Scripture warns believers to save their precious time by not getting romantically involved with the wrong people. Some believers date or marry unbelievers, later to discover a counterfeit love that leads to separation, abuse, neglect, rejection, and sometimes divorce. It is important to find out what true love is so our time is not wasted on counterfeit love. The Lord never intended for us to forsake Him for the sake of loving someone else. Even if you develop an intimate relationship with another believer, you should be able to discern if your partner's first love is God. Is that person seeking God and depending on Him? Is he or she submitting to God and His Word? If your beloved is not fully committed to God in this way, then I would caution you to carefully consider if this person truly loves you the way God desires for you to be loved.

What if believers invested their time in getting to know God and made it their priority to pursue God as their first love? Then, their focus will be on God and not on other things or people. Then, everyone and everything will be placed in their proper order. The most important commandment is to love God with all your heart, with all your soul, with all your mind, and with all your strength (Matthew 22:37). God requires believers to love Him wholeheartedly: He should be esteemed higher than any person or object. God must not be second to anything or anyone.

Some believers get caught up in pursuing a person or a relationship and forget that their top priority should be to seek first the kingdom of God and His righteousness. God knows best: He knows that if we do not seek Him first, then other people and things will compete with our time for Him. Do not be misled into placing your affection or devotion on a person or thing instead of God, creating an idol for yourself.

Mark 12:32 says that the second most important commandment is, "Love your neighbor as yourself." Notice that Jesus said that we are to love God first; then we are to love our neighbors second. God wants His children to show *agape* love to everyone, regardless of who they are, in the same way that He loves.

At the same time, we must choose not to associate with things or people who can influence us to turn away from our first love or sin against Him. First John 2:15 says, "Do not love the world or anything in the world. If anyone loves the world, the love of the Father is not in him. For everything in the world—the cravings of sinful man, the lust of his eyes and the boasting of what he has and does—comes not from the Father but from the world." The world wants us to have fellowship with it and be devoted to its values, pleasures, and lifestyles.

Some believers include a wide variety of activities in their daily schedules that cater to the sinful nature—the lust of the eyes and the lust of the flesh. The most important thing for us to do as believers, however, is to spend time seeking God first; then our focus will be on His true love that can fill the void in our lives which causes us to search for other worldly things.

Remember that God created us to live in two realms: the natural and the supernatural. God wants us to live *in* the world, but not be *of* the world. As long as we're alive, we will have a sinful nature, but we who are born of God have become partakers of His divine nature, since God is within us (2 Peter 1:4). When we are seeking to know God, we realize that we are intertwined with His Spirit who lives in us; therefore, we possess His very nature within our spirits.

God has always loved His people, even before the foundations of the world. He already had a plan to provide the Lamb slain on our behalf so that we would not have to remain in a fallen state. We now have the way through the redemptive power of Christ to receive salvation of our souls which both secures forgiveness for our sins and restores us to a right relationship with Him. God's love is revealed to us and the world through His Son Jesus, who sacrificed Himself for us by dying on the cross for our sins, so that any one of us who believes in His finished work on the cross may be saved (John 3:16-18).

To really know God, we need to know His Word. John 1:1 says, "In the beginning was the Word, and the Word was with God, and the Word was God." Because God and His Word are one, He reveals His character through His Word.

I wanted to know God for myself, so I began to read and study the Bible. I soon learned that God was faithful to His people all through the Bible. On many occasions, God demonstrated His faithfulness by His divine protection, healing, deliverance, intervention, and provision. David experienced firsthand His loving kindness, faithfulness, compassion, mercy, and forgiveness. The more I read about the Lord and how He relates to people in the Bible, the more I want to know what is on His heart, just as I would try to find out the likes and dislikes of a person whom I'm trying to get to know. I find myself wanting to please God and do nice things for Him like I desire to do in a close earthly relationship.

God knows His children: He is always looking for opportunities to prepare us to receive a blessing from Him. How many times have we said, "Lord, you sure did bless me today," or "Lord, you knew exactly what I needed!"? We show our love for the Lord daily by spending time with Him, finding out what He wants us to do for Him, and then obeying Him. If we love Him, then we will obey Him. The more time I spend with the Lord, the more I want to do His will and devote myself entirely to Him.

I have read about the lives of three particular people in the Bible who have helped me to see how God reveals Himself: Enoch, David, and the apostle Paul. Enoch found time to walk with God daily. The Word of God says that, "By faith Enoch was taken from this life, so that he did not experience death; he could not be found, because God had taken him away. For before he was taken, he was commended as one who pleased God" (Hebrews 11:5). It blessed me that the Lord desired such personal fellowship with Enoch, and he responded by seeking an intimate relationship with God.

I desire to know God like Enoch, and He has honored my request by drawing me closer to Himself, making me one with Him. How much closer can I get? Closer. During my breathtaking times of refreshing that I spend with the Lord, He reveals Himself to me in wonderful, new ways. I have learned His strategy, wisdom, and plans for managing my time, and it never ceases to amaze me how He manages to increase my time supernaturally to do more for the kingdom.

Another biblical figure I studied was David, a man after God's own heart. Because he loved the Lord so much, he was quick to repent from the sins that he had committed against Him. David spent a great deal of time alone with the Lord while he was a shepherd attending his father's sheep. In return, God revealed Himself mightily to David. David knew Him personally as his deliverer and protector, especially when God rescued him from the deadly paws of the lion and the bear (I Samuel 17:37).

David had acquired not just head knowledge but also revelation knowledge of who God was. He had begun to experience the Lord in many ways, especially by His faithfulness in delivering Goliath into his hands. I want to be like David—a servant after God's own heart.

Often during my prayer times, the Lord reveals things that are dear to His heart. He has given me an assignment to pray for the body of Christ so that we would know who we are in Christ Jesus, who Christ Jesus is, and the resurrection power which raised Christ from the dead that now lives in our hearts. When we get this revelation knowledge, then we will live in triumph over the enemies of God. Because this desire was dear to the heart of God, I received that prayer assignment as dear to my heart as well. I strongly desired to touch the heart of God with my prayers.

The apostle Paul was the other biblical person I studied. He had revelation knowledge of the deep things of God. I appreciate how Paul encouraged the believers to walk by faith and not by sight because it is impossible to please

God without faith. Paul chose to live by faith and by the Word of God. I have chosen to live my life by faith in God and His Word. I told God that I wanted to exercise my faith to do what He was calling me both to do and become. He has responded by giving me many opportunities to not only grow in my faith but also to share it with others.

God turned Paul's life around to help others walk in faith. He became a doer of the Word and demonstrated Christ-like character throughout his ministry. Likewise, my desire is to know the Lord and allow His Word to renew my mind so that I can receive revelation knowledge of who I am in Christ Jesus and then demonstrate the character of Christ to others. To know God is to know His Son Christ Jesus, who is our role model for knowing, loving, and serving our heavenly Father.

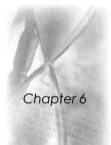

Chapter 6

JESUS IS OUR ROLE MODEL

J esus is the exact representation of God; He is the visible image of the invisible God (Colossians 1:15). Jesus is our role model for how we should love God. God first loved us by giving "His one and only Son, that whoever believes in Him shall not perish but have eternal life" (John 3:16). Jesus gave His life for us so that we will be saved and set free from the penalty of sin and the power of sin. "Greater love has no one than this, that he lay down his life for his friends" (John 15:13).

Jesus modeled love for us by loving both God the Father and us. He not only gave us a command to love one another, but He lived it out while He was on this earth. Jesus also said that if we love Him, we will obey His commands (John 15:10). Jesus spent His time loving people who did not love Him first. How much more should we love Him and then love one another? The Word of God says that they will know that we are His disciples by our love for one another. Love requires that we give. How much are we giving to others with our acts of kindness—helping those who need help and encouraging those who are discouraged? How much of ourselves are we giving to others without complaining?

God is making a demand on what He has already given through His precious Son. Jesus said in John 15:9-10, "As the Father has loved me, so have I loved you. Now remain in my love. If you obey my commands, you will remain in my love, just as I have obeyed my Father's commands and remain in His love." Jesus made His example of love for the Father very clear by obeying His commands.

Jesus not only loved the Father but He also submitted himself to the authority of God. Jesus modeled how we should act under the authority of God. The Greek word for authority is *exousia*, which means the right to exercise power, while *dunamis* is the Greek word for power, which means ability, abundance, and strength. Authority is the right to do what is legal, lawful, and right with the expressed backing of the one who is sending him. If a police officer stops a car and shows the driver his badge, for example, he is letting him know that he is authorized to tell him to pull over. If the driver does not stop, he has the gun (the *dunamis* power) to enforce it.

In Luke 4:36, Jesus used His authority against demonic spirits and then backed it up with the *dunamis*, the miracle-working power of God, to enforce it. *Exousia* and *dunamis* are the twin weapons that we have in our arsenal to battle against the works of Satan. Because Jesus Himself was under the authority of His Father, He was also able to exercise authority over the works of the enemy. This authority was delegated to Jesus as a man, but He moved with the authority of God the Father in the power of the Holy Spirit. In Matthew 8:5-9, the centurion told Jesus that he also was a man under authority like Him. His soldiers were subject to him, so they obeyed his commands. Jesus came to earth as a man both under authority and with authority.

In Matthew 7:28, it says that the people were amazed at His teachings because He taught as one who had authority. We need to follow the example that Jesus gave us. To receive authority from God, we should obey His authority over us.

In Acts 19:13-17, the sons of Jewish chief priest Sceva were trying to drive out evil spirits. They were not under authority because they did not have a relationship with Jesus; therefore, they could not exercise authority either. The demonic spirits knew that they did not belong to Jesus, so they were able to easily overpower them.

Authority comes with boundaries. We are constrained by the Bible, and our scope is determined by the Word of God. Some believers who want to do their own thing operate outside the bounds of the authority delegated to them, which is unwise. If we operate outside the scope of authority over us, God will not back us up with His power. If we do not submit to the authorities that He has placed over us, then how can we exercise authority over the works of the enemy?

Jesus also modeled for us how to resist temptation from Satan by using the Word of God against him. Satan used part of the Scriptures out of context to tempt Jesus to sin against God, but Jesus quoted the Word of God back to him, thereby resisting the temptation. Satan was trying to distort the truth of God's Word, but Jesus was not deceived. James 4: 7 says, "Submit yourselves therefore to God. Resist the devil, and he will flee from you" (KJV). Jesus resisted all the appeals of Satan by quoting the Word of God and acting in obedience to His Father's will. Temptation is an invitation to sin against God, but we do not have to accept it.

Satan tried to tempt Jesus in three areas described in 1 John 2:16: "For all that is in the world, the lust of the flesh, and the lust of the eyes, and the pride of life, is not of the Father, but is of the world" (KJV). Satan also used these three areas of temptation with Eve in the Garden to mislead her into transgressing against God. When Jesus was tempted, however, Satan was unable to deceive him, so he did not sin against God.

Satan appeals to the weakness of the flesh—especially by awakening desires through the eyes—but also through pride. That's why it is important to take the time to renew our mind by studying the Word of God. It will have a direct influence over both our will and emotions; then we will act according to the Spirit of God guiding us instead of allowing our flesh to dictate our behavior. As believers, we must know the Word of God thoroughly in order to recognize when the Word of God is taken out of context or mixed with partial truth in deceptive attempts to persuade us to do something wrong.

Satan will try to tempt us in these areas, just as he did with Eve and Jesus. Our response should be like the one Jesus gave him: "It is written." We need to know the Word and quote it when we are tempted. Then, we should continue to submit to God, and the devil will flee for a period of time. We must keep up our guard because he will try to tempt us again, always probing to see if we are still submitting ourselves to God and standing on the Word. First Peter 5: 8-9 states, "Be self-controlled and alert. Your enemy the devil prowls around like a roaring lion looking for someone to devour. Resist him, standing firm in the faith, because you know that your brothers throughout the world are undergoing the same kind of sufferings."

Jesus is also our ultimate role model for bringing our personal time under control. Jesus spent a great deal of time daily with God to receive His agenda for that day. Jesus was *mission-minded*: he spent His time on earth fulfilling the mission that was set before Him by the Father. Luke 19:10 says, "For the Son of man is come to seek and to save that which was lost" (KJV). Jesus came to earth to bring the lost into His kingdom. He was *kingdom-minded*: He preached about the kingdom; He advanced His kingdom by making disciples who carried out the Great Commission, and He also came to destroy the works of the devil.

Jesus modeled for us how we should work for the kingdom. Not only did Jesus preach the gospel pertaining to the kingdom, but He also went about doing good for the kingdom, healing all that were oppressed by the devil, for God was with Him (Acts 10:38). Jesus came to confront the kingdom of darkness with His kingdom of light. Not only was Jesus the light of the world, but He also showed *us* how to be the light of the world. Those who are in the world living in darkness are looking for us who have the light to show them the way to Christ Jesus.

Jesus was able to accomplish more in His three and a half years of ministry than many of us try to do in our entire lifetime. Jesus did not commit His time to do things other than the will of God. John 4:34 says that Jesus' purpose was to do the will of the Father and finish His work that He started on earth. Jesus submitted His will to do the will of the Father, even to the point of dying on the cross and being separated from Him by taking on the sins of the whole world. John 5:30 says that Jesus did not seek His own will but the will of the Father who sent Him.

Time Management, God's Way will require us to follow Christ's example for submitting our will to the Father's will. There are times when I know that the Lord is telling me to do something that I do not want to do, but I have to say, "Not my will be done, but Your will be done." When I spend time doing what God has ordained me to do, I am able to complete my ministry assignments. I find myself developing a single-minded focus for doing *only* what is on God's agenda for that day.

Jesus said in John 5:19, "I tell you the truth, the Son can do nothing by himself; he can do only what he sees his Father doing, because whatever the Father does the Son also does." Jesus rose early in the morning while it was still dark and went to a solitary place to spend time in prayer with His Father to see what He had already planned for Him to do (Mark 1:35). Jesus modeled His lifestyle of prayer and intimacy with the Father for us to imitate.

Jesus did not have to be concerned about someone else giving Him an agenda because He knew the Creator who made all things. Jesus took the time to seek God first by communing with Him on a daily basis. This resulted in Jesus the Son manifesting the thoughts of God the Father through miracles He performed on earth. In Matthew 14:15-21, for example, Jesus saw what God had already done in heaven and came into agreement with His will to be done on earth when he trusted Him to provide food for more than five thousand hungry people. Jesus had already taught His disciples how to pray in the Sermon on the Mount: "Our Father in heaven, hallowed be your name, your kingdom come, your will be done on earth as it is in heaven."

We also need to follow Jesus Christ's example of cultivating a lifestyle of prayer—not just occasionally praying when we are faced with difficult situations. Many times, we look first to others who only have a limited understanding of our problem and inadequate resources to meet our needs. Instead, we should seek the King first who owns everything and wants to take care of His children. This is why Matthew 6:33 is so important—it requires us to seek both His kingdom and His righteousness to receive our blessing. In the same way that Jesus trusted His Father to multiply two fish and five loaves of bread to feed the vast multitude of people, we need to trust the Father to multiply our time and give us the increase to put back into His kingdom. When Jesus received this huge increase of food, He did not hoard it up for Himself for a rainy day, but instead he invested it in kingdom work, which is the will of God.

When I spend time with God early in the morning, it orders the priorities of my day according to God's schedule, and I choose to submit to His timetable. I get more done supernaturally with an increase of time because the grace of God is assisting me to accomplish His will and purpose for my life. He once reminded me that His grace is here to help us to accomplish His will—not our own.

Jesus also showed us how important it is to spend time with Him so that we can be refreshed in His presence. When Jesus was ministering to the people, at some point He needed to find time to get away from the crowd to be alone with His Father. Likewise, there are times when the Lord calls me to a place of rest in Him. At one time in my life, I found myself at the point of being emptied of the rivers of living water flowing out of me. Jesus desired for me to come unto Him to receive rest and drink from the fountains of living water that were only found in Him. The Lord cautioned me to no longer minister out of self, but to minister out of the overflow of the Spirit.

Jesus modeled for us a lifestyle of spending time alone with the Father, which allowed him to be refreshed to accomplish more in His ministry. Jesus says in Matthew 11:28-30, "Come to me, all you who are weary and burdened, and I will give you rest. Take my yoke upon you and learn from me, for I am gentle and humble in heart, and you will find rest for your souls. For my yoke is easy and my burden is light." When we yoke up with the Lord, we will find our work not to be as hard. We will actually have a light workload, which will give us more time to do other things with a spirit of ease.

I've often experienced times when the Lord desires to deposit a divine impartation into my spirit. There are other times when I get quiet to hear Him speak to me about many areas of my life, such as new assignments, areas of weakness that need to be exchanged for His strength, character defects that need to be transformed by the Word of God, temptations that are heading my way so I can look for the way of escape, and new challenges to stretch my faith.

There are so many things that the Lord speaks into my life, in addition to receiving more of His power as I come under the authority of His Word. Jesus came to give life and give it more abundantly (John 10:10). When I receive this life, it is the *zoe*, a Greek word meaning the "God-kind of life." Along with it comes the characteristic traits of God that make us partakers of His divine nature. To put it simply, the more time I spend with Him, the more I become like Him. First Corinthians 2:16 says that we have the mind of Christ, so it behooves us to take the time to cultivate intimacy with Him to know what is on His mind.

Jesus also modeled for us how to serve one another. God the Father prepared a body for Jesus to dwell in while He was on earth. Then, Jesus emptied Himself of His glory, majesty, power, and dignity, but not His divinity. In other words, Jesus was both completely human and completely divine (John 1:1, 14).

This act was called *kenosis* in the Greek, meaning "emptying oneself." This *kenosis* is clearly shown in Philippians 2:5-8, that describes Jesus leaving His glory in heaven to take on the humiliating position of a servant, becoming obedient to death for the benefit of all. Jesus modeled servanthood to those He served. In Matthew 20:28, it says that "the Son of man did not come to be served, but to serve, and to give his life as a ransom for many."

When a dispute arose among the disciples over who was the greatest (Luke 22:26-27), Jesus taught them that lording it over someone else does not define greatness; instead, serving others is the standard of leadership. Later, at the Last Supper recorded in John 13:1-5, He showed His disciples how to serve one another by His selfless example of washing their feet.

We can compare Jesus laying aside His garments, which represents Him taking off His authority, majesty, dignity, and power, and putting on the garb of a servant to His act of taking on human form to serve mankind. If Jesus was willing to humble Himself to serve us, then we should also be willing to serve God and one another.

Jesus had to remind His disciples by example that by serving God first, He served mankind. Moreover, He showed them His willingness to do any act of kindness and service for them through the simple act of washing their feet. He wanted them to understand that their desire to be superior than their fellow disciples was contrary to the spirit of being a servant that He had just demonstrated.

True greatness involves us serving God and doing His will; then, others will reap the benefits. God gave us an example of how we should serve Him and others through His Son Jesus Christ. As servants of God, we should never lose sight of our vision. We can be confident in knowing that the Father will give us a plan to serve Him and others, just as He did for Jesus.

God has plans for our lives to prosper us in ways that are far better than our ways or the world's ways of doing things. Because His ways are much higher than our ways, we as believers need to take the time to discover the blueprints for our lives from the One who knows the end from the beginning.

Chapter 7

GOD HAS PLANS FOR OUR LIVES

Have you ever had plans, but they did not prosper? When you made these plans, did you humbly submit them to the Lord to see if He wanted you to pursue them?

The Lord desires for us to seek Him first before we commit to plans that may lead to an unproductive, unsuccessful, discouraging, and sometimes destructive outcome. The Lord makes it clear in Jeremiah 29:11 that He will watch over His beneficial plans for us and bring them to pass. Can we truly say that the plans we make without consulting the Lord will prosper us?

Proverbs 16:3 says, "Commit to the Lord whatever you do, and your plans will succeed." When we seek the Lord first concerning the plans that He already has for us, then His plans will become our plans. Our plans should be in harmony with His kingdom and His truth.

During my time with the Lord, He showed me the importance of spending time with Him first regarding the plans He has for us. By doing this, I began to see that how we allocate time to carry out our goals, projects, and ministries is important to Him. God reminded me that since He is the giver of time, He desires for us to get in His presence so that we will have His mindset concerning our agenda for that day. When I come before Him, I spend quality time to learn His Word by reading, studying, and meditating on it. Then, I take time alone with Him to see what He wants to say to me.

God began to rearrange my agenda according to the blueprint that had already been planned out for my life, according to 1 Corinthians 2:9-10: "But as it is written, Eye hath not seen, nor ear heard, neither have entered the heart of man, the things which God hath prepared for them that love him. But God hath revealed them unto us by his Spirit: for the Spirit searcheth all things, yea, the deep things of God" (KJV).

My life blueprint is designed especially to help me carry out the assignments given to me by God to build up and advance His kingdom. Our goals and pursuit of success in life should be based on spiritual things such as the kingdom of God, not on earthly things that are temporary and subject to change and corruption.

God placed on my heart that only His eternal purposes for our lives would satisfy the void in our hearts. When we seek to fulfill His plans, we will live purpose-driven lives that are directed by the Lord, who is our ultimate time manager.

If we do not pursue the Lord's eternal purposes for our lives, then we will waste time filling our lives with trivial things. When this happens, we will never be satisfied because we are not doing what we were created to do. There are too many people walking around aimlessly without a purpose in life who are bored, frustrated, angry, and depressed because they are living a counterfeit life instead of the abundant life that Jesus Christ came to give them. Satan tries to deceive us into thinking that we are living life to the fullest, but actually we are living mediocre lives in comparison to what the Lord has already planned for us.

In my own life, I discovered that it was not too late to seek the Lord about His plans for me, even though I had made mistakes in the past. I chose to develop a lifestyle of seeking God first and spending time with Him to get His agenda and plans for my life. Once I submitted to this process, I was able to see the Lord's vision for where He was taking me before I set out to do it.

The Lord gave me a vision to carry out His plans and purposes for my life according to His kingdom principles. He showed me a two-fold plan: one is the strategic or long-term plan that involves the overall implementation at a certain point in time, and the other one is the tactical or short-range plan—the practical arm consisting of a series of short-term projects assigned by the Lord to accomplish His vision. (The Lord also has ordained other people to help us to carry out the vision so that we will not get overwhelmed.)

Once I embark upon these plans, I will see the vision fulfilled, slowly but surely, because it cannot happen all at once. If the Lord showed us everything that He desires for us to do, it would exhaust us; therefore, He gives us many different assignments to do over a long period of time.

I am also learning how to sense when my assignment is finished. If my task is completed, I gradually end up struggling with the assignment, and the joy of doing it is no longer there. When the Spirit of grace, the Holy Spirit, is empowering me to accomplish a task for the Lord, then I will experience His peace while doing it.

For this season of my life, the Lord has defined His vision for me. The strategic plan covered developing my personal devotion to the Lord and my family; practicing my daily disciplines that help me to grow spiritually; getting involved with ministries at my church; exercising my faith daily; working on my job as unto the Lord; ministering effectively just where I am, and attending Bible college.

The Lord also desired for me to continue the ministry of intercessory prayer, which included praying for the body of Christ to be sensitive to His voice, His presence, and His prodding. The other assignment was to pray that we would receive a greater revelation of who we are in Christ Jesus.

When I received this strategic plan for my life, I immediately came into agreement with it. I have chosen to exercise my faith, believing that God's grace would help me achieve all that He was calling me to do. All I have had to do is my part, and the Holy Spirit has empowered me to do the rest. It's a good thing that He gave me a short-range plan to achieve these goals and projects, or I would have been quickly overwhelmed. I spent much time in prayer so that the Lord could give me a framework in which to operate.

Everything that God gives us involves potential that must be developed and cultivated to turn it into full reality. It was not enough for me just to think about the vision; I had to use practical planning to bring it to pass. I needed time, effort, and determination, along with the help of the Holy Spirit.

Each day, I spent quality time with the Lord to hear what He had to say about my daily agenda. I always asked Him what I should do first and then how I should do it. Now that I had the strategy, I had to implement the next part of the plan, which involved carrying out the long-term tactics of the vision He had given me.

This tactical plan was simply gaining a practical sense of committing my time to the Lord in every area of my life. He instructed me through His Word to write down the vision so that I could see where He was taking me. Habakkuk 2:2-3 states, "And the Lord answered me, and said, Write the vision, and make it plain upon tables, that he may run that readeth it. For the vision is yet for an appointed time, but at the end it shall speak, and not lie: though it tarry, wait for it; because it will surely come, it will not tarry" (KJV). I began doing this by writing the dates of my ministry meetings at church on the calendar. (Our small group meetings at the church were scheduled two months in advance, with each leader committing to their designated date in the rotation.)

Once I committed myself to these dates, I asked God to protect my time of ministry unto Him, and He honored my request. I didn't have any overlapping scheduled appointments, but if I had any, those that were already on the calendar were the ones that the Lord wanted me to give priority to, because He had showed me what was important to Him. Committing my time first to the Lord allowed me to develop some Christlike character traits in my life. Once I submitted to this process, I became reliable, dependable, consistent, and faithful with the projects the Lord gave me to do.

I started out by attending Sunday school and regular church services consistently, then Bible study, prayer meetings, and other ministry meetings on a regular basis. People were able to depend on me to be there on time and do all that was asked of me.

Because I desire to work as unto the Lord, I also committed the time on my job to Him. The Lord will give us various opportunities to develop the Christlike character traits of faithfulness, dependability, and trustworthiness as a witness to others in the workplace. As imitators of Christ, we should allow God to transform us into His image.

The Lord always desires for His children to succeed in all that He has planned for us to do in our lifetime. When people look at our good works, they will know that we serve the living God, and they'll give Him glory. That is part of His plan for our lives—not just to grow physically, but also to grow up spiritually in Christ Jesus. God will meet each one of us where we are. We all have different gifts, talents, and abilities that God has given us to accomplish the plans that He has for us to build up His kingdom.

We need to start by giving our time to Him so that He can manage it according to His blueprint for our lives. Psalm 139:13-16 says that He knows the plans He has for us, even before we were formed in our mother's womb. Sometimes we do not know where to begin, so we do not even start: we do nothing. One thing I have learned is that the Holy Spirit, who is our helper, will not jump-start our work. He will come alongside of us to empower us to do the will of God, but we have to start from where we are.

Remember that exercising our faith to do the will of God will give us access to His grace to help us do all that He calls us to do. God desires for us to succeed—never to fail.

There was a time when I asked the Lord, "Where do I start in doing Your will for my life?" The Lord showed me to start with whatever I was comfortable doing. Ecclesiastes 9:10 states, "Whatever your hand finds to do, do it with all your might." That is what I began to do. I started out by helping in the children's choir because as a mother of two daughters, I was comfortable working with children. God reminded me that if we are faithful over the little that He gives us to do, then He would allow us to be faithful over many things that He has already ordained for us to do in the future. The parable of the talents found in Matthew 25:14-30 shows us that God wants us to be good stewards over all that He has given us—our abilities, time, resources, and opportunities—so that we can serve Him well while we are on earth. God will then give us opportunities to use these gifts to continue doing kingdom work in heaven.

Once I became faithful with my time, then I learned to use my gifts and resources for God. I developed consistency with giving offerings and eventually became faithful to return the tithe back to the Lord. Later, I committed myself to sharing my resources. I opened my home to host small group ministry meetings, and later on, to serve the people of God through one-on-one discipleship, prayer, and edification.

The Lord's plan is for us to be saved and become a member of His kingdom, submit to His lordship, and learn from His Word how to live according to His righteous standards. Once we start to grow and mature in Him, the Lord wants us to serve Him and others, advancing His kingdom by carrying out the Great Commission.

When we are faithful over a few tasks that the Lord has given us, then we qualify to be faithful over many things. God showed me how this worked in my own life. After I consistently helped with the children's choir, He opened up other ministry opportunities for me, such as serving in the Prayer Ministry and teaching a Sunday school class. I especially enjoyed teaching because when I studied my lesson plans, I developed a consuming passion for the Word of God, which later helped me to embrace the call to attend Bible college.

As you can see, I accomplished these ministry tasks by obeying the small tactical projects or assignments designed by the Lord for me to develop character and growth in specific areas of my faith. This assisted me in becoming a role model for others—especially for my daughters.

When I was asked to be an assistant leader in the small group ministry at our church, I came up with all types of excuses for not becoming a leader because I did not see myself as a leader at the time. Later on, however, after spending time with the Lord and His Word, I found out who I truly was in Christ Jesus.

When we don't know who we are in Christ, we can disqualify ourselves from achieving our destiny in Him because we lack the confidence that we can do everything that He calls us to do through His grace. Wasting time doing things that are not a part of God's plan for our lives will only leave us frustrated and still searching for things to do with our time.

After I relinquished my time to God and allowed Him to set priorities in my life, then I became eager to accomplish what He gave me to do. Now, my gifts could make room for me to minister with each open door of opportunity that was given to me.

Sometimes we manage our time with a small view of the future that is planned out for us by God. We must seek God's kingdom first so that we can develop a kingdom mindset to get the big picture of God's eternal purposes for us. As believers, we should strive toward seeking His will for our lives because our prosperity lies in His plans and not our own.

Are you managing your time according to God's plans or your plans? When you realize that God wants to prosper you and plans to give you a future and a hope, then you will desire to spend time with Him to know His will for your life. God's plans by far supersede your own plans. When you begin to see things from God's perspective, you can better appreciate the awesome and vast plans He has for you. God will then give you His grace to help you live a life of abundance.

I did not realize that my life of ministry would start with the children's choir and spread into areas that I had never dared to consider before. I also did not know that I could handle several ministries at the same time, but the Holy Spirit has directed me with His steady guidance.

As I learned to manage my time in being faithful over all that the Lord gave me to do, He called me to go to Bible college. At the same time, He was also leading me to do missionary work in Haiti. I must admit that I felt like the Lord was asking me to do too many things at one time. He also was stretching my faith to believe that He would provide for two areas of ministry that would require finances I did not have at the time. During my prayer time with the Lord, I shared my concerns about not being able to do what He was calling me to do. (I am so thankful that we can always go straight to the throne of God with open hearts and be transparent with Him about any fears or misunderstandings that we may have.)

The Lord asked me two questions: "Are you willing? Are you available?" My response was, "Yes, I am willing and available." It is not my *ability* that the Lord was looking for, but my *availability*. The Lord told me, "Then, go." That was His Great Commission placed before me, and I received it. I have chosen to obey God with both of the assignments that He has given me.

God is looking for us to agree with what He is saying about us or what He wants us to do. Then, not only will He give us His vision for our lives, but He will also go ahead of us and provide for the vision: it is called provision. Without having everything in place, I had to take a step of faith to allow the Lord to finance both assignments: attending Bible college and going on mission trips to Haiti. When I said "yes" to His will, the Lord made a way out of "no way." Many times, we have our own vision for our lives but lack the financial provision to bring it to pass. If it is His vision, then He will provide the "pro-vision." Notice that "pro" goes before the "vision." Though the vision may tarry, the Lord will bring it to pass at the appointed time.

The Lord so graciously provided a way for me to pay for the four years of Bible college, and I graduated as an ordained, licensed minister. He also supplied enough funds to go on the mission trips to Haiti. My first trip was completely funded by the people of God who were moved by His Spirit to bless me financially to cover my expenses. Since then, I have gone on four mission trips to Haiti, for which the Lord provided me with funds through faithful members of my church and friends who blessed me with airline tickets and money, as well as supplies for the native people. Each mission trip was a walk of faith.

The Lord continued to confirm the tactical plans that He wanted me to carry out after I committed my time to Him and came into agreement with all that He desired for me to do. I just needed to look at it through my spiritual eyes so I could walk by faith and not by sight. Yet, I was concerned about doing so many things while others were only doing a few things or nothing at all.

I went before the Lord in prayer regarding this situation. The next day while I was attending a class at Bible college, my instructor stopped in the middle of his lesson and said that the Holy Spirit was leading him to share a specific word concerning someone in the class. He said that "someone here had asked the Lord why they should do more than anyone else." He reminded us of the parable of the talents, which revealed how the Lord entrusted His grace to those whom He called. My instructor continued. "Some have the grace on their lives to do ten things, while others have the grace operating on their lives to accomplish only one thing. If you have the grace of God operating on your life to do ten things, it is better for you to be obedient to do the ten things the Lord has called you to do rather than five or even one thing."

"Also, the Lord may have given someone else the grace to do only one thing. It's better for that person to use the grace on his life to do that one thing instead of trying to do two or more things with the amount of grace given him to cover just the one thing. The grace of God is supernatural ability given to us to help us accomplish His purposes, not our purpose," he concluded.

I began to repent right there in class and purposed in my heart to do what God called me to do. Even though His grace was going to help me do it, I needed more than ever to spend time seeking Him first to get His game plan to achieve the goals He had set out before me.

When anxiety tries to overtake me with questions such as, *How will I do it?* and *Where will I get the money to do it?*, I choose to believe that the Lord is faithful to His promise in Matthew 6:33. I decided to do my part in seeking God first and His righteousness, allowing Him to prioritize my time to accomplish all my ministry duties at the church, along with any additional assignments in my personal life. Certainly, the Lord is faithful to do His part by giving me all that I need to accomplish His goals and plans for my life as well as multiplying my time so that I can sow it back into His kingdom.

This spiritual principle had a profound meaning for me because it prepared me to exercise my faith by believing that God would provide for me during my four years of Bible college and for my mission trips to Haiti. I have learned that when the Lord gives you a vision to follow for your life, He will also give you provision to take you through the process.

I made up my mind that if God had called me to do these assignments, then He already had that time allotted for me to accomplish them for the kingdom of God. Once I came into agreement with what He had assigned me to do, then He was able to make all grace abound to me, so that in all things at all times, having all that I need, I would abound in every good work (2 Corinthians 9:8).

God showed me that when I allow Him to manage my time, then I do not have to worry about how His assignment for me is going to get done. All I had to do was trust Him, and He would provide. I learned a valuable lesson during this walk of faith: the just shall walk by faith and not by sight. God never intended for us to walk any other way except by faith because without faith it is impossible to please God (Hebrews 11:6).

I hope that you have received some insight from this chapter about depending on the Lord to give you the plans that He has already ordained for you. He said that He knew us before we were in our mother's womb. The Lord's plans will prosper us and not harm us and give us a hope and a future. Whose plans are defining your life—yours or the Lord's? Remember, you can start right where you are by spending time with the Lord and asking Him to reveal His plans to you. Write down the vision He gives you, understanding that the vision will not come to fruition immediately but in God's appointed time. The Lord has to first prepare us for the vision so that we may be established in what He has called us to do.

He will make our feet like hind's feet and set us upon high places (Psalms 18:33). The Lord will prepare the way for us by giving us ministry opportunities before He sends us out; therefore, it is important not to shrink back from serving in ministry. We need to just start where we are, and the Lord will meet us at that point. This preparation time may involve experiences that we may not be comfortable with, but they will force us to leave our comfort zone and trust God. These assignments may seem insignificant or tedious to us at the time, but we should do them anyway without murmuring or complaining, knowing that it is the Lord who equips us to serve—no matter how menial the task may be.

When we place our time into His hands, He not only will multiply it back with interest, but He will also protect it. We must acknowledge that the time we spend in service is accounted back to God as worship. He takes this time as a seed, gives it the increase, and returns it to us as fruit. People will then see our good works and give God the glory. This is the season when the Lord is fulfilling the good work that He began in us, because we have chosen to submit even our time to Him.

The apostle Paul confirms this truth: "For we are his workmanship, created in Christ Jesus unto good works, which God hath before ordained that we should walk in them" (Ephesians 2:10, KJV). Colossians 3:23-24 states, "And whatsoever ye do, do it heartily, as to the Lord, and not unto men; knowing that of the Lord ye shall receive the reward of the inheritance: for ye serve the Lord Christ" (KJV).

Chapter 8

TIME ROBBERS

We all are living busy lives in a very fast-paced society that is constantly demanding more and more of our time. *Time Management God's Way* will never cause us to live under pressure; by the very grace of God, we will live a stress-free life. Remember, Paul said that God is able to make all grace abound to us, so that in all things, at all times; having all that we need, we will abound in every good work (2 Corinthians 9:8).

God already has set aside the time needed for us to accomplish all that He asks us to do. Jesus, who is our role model, finished His work on this earth in three and one-half years. We can do the same in our lives, but we need to watch out for "time robbers" that challenge many of us in our busy schedules and prevent us from doing what the Lord has already planned for us to do.

Procrastination

Procrastination, the insidious habit of putting things off until the last minute, is a major time robber for many people. Throughout my life, I have been challenged with this problem area, so I knew that I had to get to its root cause in order to deal with it. I first had to admit that there was a problem.

After taking a closer look at the situation, I realized that I usually yielded to procrastination when I took on a project that I felt was too big for me to accomplish. If I looked at the huge project as a whole, I could not see myself completing it, so I would put off starting it. I would rather find time to make telephone calls, watch TV, or work on another smaller project. Also, if I could not clearly envision all the steps necessary to complete the project, I would feel overwhelmed and put it off. I began to seek the Lord for His wisdom and guidance to help me solve this problem.

The Lord reminded me that I can do all things through Him who strengthens me to complete the assignment. Even though His grace would not jump-start what I was responsible to initiate, I had to believe that the Holy Spirit would come alongside of me as a helper to give me the grace to accomplish what the Lord had asked me to do. Simply put, I had to do my part, and then the Lord would do His part. Sometimes, we forget that the Lord will not override our will to do what He desires for us to do. As an act of our will, we have to willingly say "yes" and then start the work by faith, because faith without works is dead (James 2:17).

The Lord showed me how to develop small steps to achieve completion of every task. When I gave in to procrastination while writing this book, for example, I had viewed the project from the perspective of one whole task, so it appeared too big for me to finish. But then I applied the Lord's strategy of breaking down the project into small steps instead of looking at the project as a whole.

During my prayer time with the Lord, I first received the layout, then the chapters, and finally the content of the book. I had to trust God that the good work He started in me He would bring to pass. In fact, this entire process helped me to exercise my faith muscles. I was faced with these questions: "How will I write the book?" and "After I write it, who will help me type it?" I knew that I could depend on my sister Jacquie and some of my friends who have blessed me by typing my papers and thesis while attending four years of Bible college, but this was a bigger project. "Who would proof and edit my book, checking it for clarity and validity?" "What about the publisher?" "How would I pay for it?" All of these questions were legitimate, but the Lord told me not to be concerned—just to trust Him and believe that He had the resources and people in place to help me finish the project. The Lord reminded me of several friends who had the ability and wisdom of God to help me in those areas of concern.

Ephesians 4:16 states, "From him the whole body, joined and held together by every supporting ligament, grows and builds itself up in love, as each part does its work." Each joint supplies the needs of others in the body of Christ. It is a blessing to have committed friends who are willing to use the gifts, talents, and abilities that the Lord gave them to help another member of the body accomplish the goals that they were assigned to do by the Lord. I just had to exercise my faith, expecting God's grace to help me accomplish what He already ordained for me to do.

Time Management God's Way is an important subject that the Lord wants His people to understand and then apply its principles in order to live an abundant, prosperous, and stress-free life. When I began to see things from the Lord's perspective, I realized that I could not only write this book as I was led by the Lord, but also to finish the project—not in my strength, but in the strength of the Lord. Those things that appeared to be impossible were now made possible with the Lord. I had to believe that in my heart and then do the work by faith. When the Lord showed me how to handle this project by breaking it down into smaller portions over a period of time, then I was able to handle it. Writing the book was a less intimidating prospect with this method.

When you receive a big assignment, ask the Lord to give you a plan on how to break it down. After you get His strategy on how to do this, commit to working on it a few minutes every day. By the end of the week, you will see some progress in your attempt to accomplish the assignment. Once you get interested in the task, you may be motivated to spend more time on it.

When I started to put the framework of my subject matter on paper, I got excited about what I would hear from the Lord, read in the Bible, or draw from my experiences; each one of these aspects helped me to override the nagging feelings to "put it off until later." In the beginning, it was a struggle, but I chose to seek God each day for His help and direction to continue writing instead of allowing procrastination to cause me to stop.

Committing to write this book allowed me to see that I could overcome all my fears that were trying to keep me from writing. The fear of failure, the fear of success, and the fear of not knowing all the mechanics of writing a book were bombarding me all at one time, but the Lord silenced each one with His Word: "The Lord did not give [me] a spirit of fear, but of power, love and a sound mind" (2 Timothy 1:7, KJV). The more time I spent with the Lord when fear tried to grip me, the more the Lord assured me that I could do all things that He called me to do through Christ Jesus who strengthened me (Philippians 4:13). The Holy Spirit empowered me to overcome the fear that was trying to overtake me, and I continued writing. I chose to keep my focus on the Lord and decrease with humility so that the life of Christ in me would increase and do the work through me.

When you have a big task and procrastination tries to keep you from starting or you cannot envision its completion, remember that you can do all things through Christ Jesus who strengthens you. The Lord will meet you where you are; just start the work by faith. Continue to seek the Lord for His wisdom, guidance, direction, and strategy on how to downsize the project into smaller steps. The Lord will send you help. His grace will enable you to do what you cannot do in your own strength. Just do your part, and then the Spirit of grace will do His part.

Distractions

Distractions are big time robbers. They get your focus off of what you should be doing and can turn you away from your present course of action. People can be a distraction when they call you or try to get you involved in unnecessary activity that will take you away from your project. If you do not spend time with the Lord to see where He is leading you, then you will not recognize the distractions when they come your way.

Have you ever received phone calls that got you stirred up and embroiled in situations that you had no business getting involved with? What is worse is hearing the Lord tell you that you are not supposed to waste your time getting involved with that situation because it wasn't your assignment. This means that His grace will not help you do what He did not call you to do.

I am learning how to stay focused on what I am supposed to be involved with instead of letting people and their agendas supersede my agenda that was prioritized by the Lord. What I am learning is that often people do not realize that we are involved with an important project, so we need to let them know about it in order for them to understand why we cannot take on another one. I've discovered that I usually get more distractions just before I teach the Word of God or when I am fasting. When distractions come, it is up to me to stay focused and continue doing what I started to do. If we do not stay focused on what is important to us, then other agendas will compete with ours and crowd out what the Lord wants us to do.

Interruptions of Thought

Interruptions of thought are distractions. Have you ever been sitting in a church service when all of a sudden these random thoughts come to your mind about things that have nothing to do with the sermon that is being preached? Your first thought is, *Where did that come from?*

These distracting thoughts can get our focus off from receiving the Word of God. It reminds me of this saying: "You may not be able to stop the birds from flying over your head, but you can stop them from making a nest on your hair." When this happens, we need to take every thought captive and make them obedient to our Lord and Savior Jesus Christ (2 Corinthians 10:5).

Satan will not only use thoughts, but he will also use people to distract us from doing the will of God or receive from Him. When distractions come, we should recognize them and continue our present course of action as directed by the Holy Spirit. If you are in your prayer time with the Lord and the phone rings twenty times, realize that it is a distraction to keep you from praying. Let the answering machine take the message, and then you can call back later. You can also let your family know if you are in a place of prayer or quiet time with the Lord so they can take a message for you.

The largest distraction since television was first introduced to our society is now the Internet, which provides a wide variety of information and sources that are helpful to persons doing research, problem-solving, and fact-finding. The problem is that people are having difficulty striking a balance with how much time they spend on the Internet.

God created all things for our use or pleasure, but sometimes we allow these things to compete with time that we should be spending with the Lord. At worst, sometimes our affection for these things has a greater priority in our lives than God, and we turn them into idols. The Lord said that we should not have any other gods before Him. It is of utmost importance for us to look at how we are spending our time. As parents, we need to check on how we are allowing our children spend their time. We should be good role models for our children because they are always watching how we live out our lives.

When children play computer games or hand-held video games, they are often greatly distracted by their content. Some games often have subtle hints of sexual perversion or an evil or violent element in them. When they are playing these games, they have difficulty paying attention to you or stopping when you ask them to stop. Sometimes, they would rather withdraw and play their video games instead of getting involved in social conversation during family time.

As parents, we need to help our children find a healthy balance in their lives by involving them in other enriching activities that will help them become well-rounded individuals. When my daughters were young, I took them to the library and museums as well as engaging them in other recreational activities that helped cultivate their God-given gifts, talents, and abilities.

We have to be careful with the Internet because even though its intended use was originally for our good, Satan always tries to pervert it to harm us. Now, many people are trying to seduce our children via the Internet into illicit sexual relationships. Myriads of pornography sites on the Internet have ruined people's lives, so we cannot allow ourselves to be passively lulled into the enemy's web of deception that tries to assure us that everything is okay with the Internet. The Internet by itself is not bad, but some of the content made available to us and our children have proven to be harmful—from bomb-making to porn.

What people may not realize is that when they allow this information into their homes, they also open a spiritual door for Satan to get a foothold into their homes.

If we believers do not use our time to seek first the kingdom of God and His righteousness, then other things will compete with time that we should spend accomplishing what the Lord has planned for us to do. Sadly, these things will only provide temporary satisfaction that will ultimately drive us to seek after something else to please us. Evil will always be around to tempt us to seek after the world's way. We must choose instead to yield ourselves to God's way, which is fulfilling the purposes that He has already ordained for our lives.

Watching Television

Watching television is a time robber that competes with time that could be spent reading, studying, and meditating on the Word of God. Many people will tell you that they don't have time to read or study the Bible because they are too busy. When you ask them how much TV they are watching, they'll confess that they spend a good portion of their time watching it. They probably don't realize that they are setting a bad example for their children who want to do the same thing most of the time.

Although I'm not a person who watches a lot of TV, now that I am born again, I only watch wholesome programs, which are few and far between. I can even get caught up watching the Christian network. The Lord once admonished me that I was spending more time viewing the praise and worship services and listening to good preaching than I was spending time with Him. I repented before the Lord because I did not want to put anything before Him, even watching the Christian network. The Christian network station is not bad in itself, but we should never let our viewing time interfere with our time of worshipping the King of kings and the Lord of lords. We desperately need balance in our lives. I am not saying that TV in itself is bad, but we do need to check the programs that we are watching and cut back on our amount of TV viewing.

When I turn off the television, I take that time to do my daily devotions, read the Word of God, pray, or get quiet before the Lord. Sometimes, I use that time to do projects that need to be done. After spending time with the Lord, I usually accomplish much more, and I am energized. When I watch TV, I have a tendency to not only get relaxed but also become lazy. Slothfulness and laziness are forerunners to poverty because we don't feel like doing anything or getting any work done. Watching TV can rob us of precious time necessary for us to succeed in completing a project, studying for an exam, doing homework, or just getting up to do something else.

Busyness

Busyness is a time robber that causes us to be busy with many activities other than what we should be doing and prevents us from having time just to be still, which is also very important. The Lord says, "Be still and know that I am God" (Psalms 46:10). In other words, drop what you're doing and do nothing. The great "I am" is present to be what we need Him to be. Sometimes we are so busy that we do not give the Lord an opportunity to show us what we should be doing for Him.

Several times, I have found myself busily doing things that were not really important. This occurred often when I started writing my book. The spirit of busyness was competing with the time that I had set aside to write. I had to decide what was a priority and what was not. Once I allowed the Lord to prioritize my schedule, then it was my responsibility to do the things that had the highest priority first and then do the other things later or not at all. I also had to learn how to say "no" to some assignments that were offered to me. It wasn't that something was wrong with these requests, but they did not fit into my schedule of priorities which I needed to accomplish. It was important for me to say "yes" to the Lord and do what He desired, instead of being a "yes person" for the sake of pleasing someone by taking on an assignment that I really could not commit to do.

I am learning not to get too busy doing my own thing, but to rather yield to the right-of-way, the Lord's way, which is the right way of doing things. Yielding our way to the Lord's way is better for us because He already knows what is going to happen during the course of the day. For instance, the Lord placed on my heart one day to rearrange my schedule so that I could do all my errands—the bank, the grocery store, the cleaners, etc.—only to see it snow the next day. By listening to the Lord, I had done all my errands in advance, so I was not anxious to get all these things done. This allowed me to have free time to spend time with the Lord in prayer, getting His strategy for an ongoing project. If we are going to be busy, we should be busy doing what has already been assigned by God for us to do. Then we will not experience stress trying to do everything at once or miss the opportunity to spend time with Him.

We can get so busy with the cares of this world that we often take our focus off Jesus who is our high priest, making intercession on our behalf. Jesus is waiting to present our petitions to the Father so that our needs can be met. Sometimes we worry ourselves into a frazzle about nothing because all of our needs have already been taken care of. We need to exercise our faith, believing that the Lord will take care of us.

That is why I appreciate what the Lord said to me at the beginning of the year: "The most important thing that my people need to do is to spend time with Me." This is what He was telling Martha in Luke 10:38-42. Martha was busy preparing a meal for Jesus because He was visiting her house. Mary chose to seize the moment, however, to be still while she sat at Jesus' feet. Mary probably enjoyed just being in His presence and sharing a rare intimate moment with Him. She may never have gotten this kind of personal time before with Jesus, perhaps because a crowd of people had always wanted Him to perform a miracle for them.

On the other hand, Martha was distracted with all her preparations, so she did not choose to sit at Jesus' feet to receive from Him and thereby missed the opportunity. Perhaps that could have been the reason why she complained, "Lord, don't you care that my sister has left me to do all the work by myself? Tell her to help me!" The exclamation point tells us that Martha may have been upset and anxious that Mary was sitting at Jesus' feet instead of helping her. But Jesus responded, "Martha, Martha, you are worried and upset about many things, but only one thing is needed. Mary has chosen what is better, and it will not be taken away from her" (Luke 10:41-42).

Jesus knew that Martha had allowed the anxiety of the moment to get the best of her. Martha had gotten so caught up with the details of preparing for Jesus that she missed the very presence of the Prince of Peace. Mary, however, chose the better way of life and peace.

It is a good thing to serve the Lord with our consistent attendance in church and active involvement in ministry and works of service. But are we so busy doing the work of the Lord that we forget to take time to be alone with Him? Doing nothing but being quiet and still so that we can hear what the Lord has to say is far better. Do we take time to learn from Him like Mary did?

The Lord will always give us an opportunity to seize the moment to sit at His feet. Will we take it?

If placed in that situation, how many of us would be so busy checking to see if the house was clean, the dinner was perfect, and everything was in its right order that when Jesus showed up we would miss the opportunity to sit at His feet and hear from Him? With my spiritual ears, I hear Jesus saying, "The most needful thing is for my people to spend time with Me."

This is a profound statement, but in its simplicity, the Lord is saying that He is waiting for us to come and sit at His feet and learn from Him. Remember, Satan would rather have us so busy that we will not have any time at all to sit and learn at Jesus' feet.

The Lord also reminded me that the cares of the world are designed to get our focus off of Him. Remember when Peter was walking on water and took his eyes off of Jesus? He began to sink as soon as he looked at the raging, stormy sea which represents the cares of the world. When the cares of the world and busyness come in to distract us, we must keep our focus on the Lord and let Him silence the storms of our lives.

In this account of Martha and Mary, the element of *worrying* brings on anxiety. Jesus said that Martha was worried about many things. Worry adds unnecessary pressure to our lives, rob us of our time, and causes us to have sleepless nights. We may not be able to do anything to change the situation, so we should let the Lord handle it instead. Why worry about something that the Lord is willing to handle Himself?

Jesus tells us in Matthew 6:25-32 not to worry about the necessities of life concerning what we will eat or wear, because our Father in heaven knows that we have need of these things. If He takes cares of the birds and the lilies of the field, how much more will He take care of the children He loves? Martha, however, had Jesus in her midst but did not know that He was the One who could take care of all of her needs.

How about you? Do you know Jesus personally as your provider? We don't want to get so busy that we miss opportunities to spend intimate moments with Jesus. Jesus desires for us to take on His yoke, which is easy, and His burden, which is light. We need to cast all of our cares—not just some of our cares—on Him, for He cares for us (1 Peter 5:7).

Clutter

Clutter is a time robber that comes into our physical space, as well as our mental space. This is a disordered state that can be found in our kitchens, closets, bedrooms, storage areas, file cabinets, and our offices. Physical clutter can add to our mental clutter because we are constantly reminded of things that need to be done, things that we cannot find, or things that we need to get rid of. Most people have clutter because they feel that they may need something one day, so they decide to hold on to it. This process continues until they run out of space, but some people just find more space to store their stuff.

When you have clutter, you usually cannot find items that you already have, so you will go to the store and buy more things. How many times have you looked in your closet or drawers to try to find something that you know you already have, but now that your space is so crowded you just cannot see it or find it? Now that you have wasted about twenty minutes trying to find it, you usually get frustrated, give up, and go purchase what you were looking for, only to go back home and later find that you already have that item. Now, you have not only wasted precious time but also your money.

This happened to me one time when I was trying to find a blue blouse in my closet, but I had so many clothes crowded in my closet that I could not find it. So I decided to take advantage of a sale at the store and purchase a blue blouse that I needed for an outfit that I was going to wear. When I returned home with the blouse that I bought, I later found the one that I was looking for. To my surprise, it turned out to be the same blouse. I was not happy. Not only did I waste my time looking for it, but I also spent money when I did not have to.

The Lord put on my heart to get rid of the clutter. I had to decide what things I really did not need, what things I could not wear, and what things I needed to donate to charity organizations or give to someone who could use them. The Lord reminded me that it was better to give away some of my clothes or other items that I did not need anymore, especially when others may need them. Our pantries or freezers can also get cluttered with food items that go way past the expiration dates. The Lord put on my heart to start checking my pantry and freezer and periodically donate the food that was still good to organizations that feed the hungry.

Not only do I choose to periodically rid clutter, but I also take the time to organize my space, because this helps me see what I actually have. Have you ever been frustrated and late for an event because you just could not find what you wanted to wear? Often I take the time to arrange my clothes in my closet, putting all the skirts together, the pants together, the blouses together, etc. This has greatly helped me to see what I have and what I need to purchase. It also saves me time in the morning because I can easily see what I can wear and pick it out with no problem. This brings order into my life, as well as helping me save time and money. When we organize our homes or workplace, we can cut down on the time needed to find something or actually do the task itself.

Our society pushes us to buy things when we really do not need anything else. We can easily stockpile, collect, hoard, and accumulate things, only to take time to get rid of them later when we run out of space or get frustrated because our space is overcrowded. The Lord does not desire for us to store up things just so we can say that we have them. We also don't have to store things up due to a concern that we will not be able to get them later when we may need them.

I have noticed that when my closets and storage areas are cluttered, it hinders me from seeing clearly in my mental space. I realized this when I was spending some time with the Lord and had difficulty seeing clearly the vision that He was giving me. Mental clutter is allowing your thoughts to run together through your mind without any particular order. When I take the time to clean out the clutter, I can see clearly where I am going with my thinking. Then, I feel relief and not frustration.

Living in the Past

Living in the past is another type of mental clutter that can rob us of our time. Have you ever thought about something that happened and you re-lived it? You vividly recall what happened, who was involved, and how you got hurt, disappointed, and angry. Replaying the experience gets you so worked up that you want to call that person and tell them how you feel.

This has happened to me on several occasions. I've only had to glance at the clock to realize that I was frozen in time. I was not doing what I started out to do, and, on top of that, I lost time by focusing on an experience that was now in the past. When we "replay the tape" of a bad memory, we also notice that our emotions are intensified in every sensitive area that has caused us some discomfort. If we are not careful, we can become depressed from reliving these traumatic experiences and prone to have emotions that make us feel like we are experiencing them over again.

We can lose precious time replaying those scenes or words over and over again in our minds, asking questions such as, "Why did it happen?" or "How come it happened to me?"

We waste too much time re-thinking it and replaying the experience by talking about it to other people like it was happening right then.

Satan does not mind us living in the past because then we are not a threat to his kingdom. He does not want us to press toward the mark of our high calling in Christ (Philippians 3:14) and become or do what the Lord has ordained for us. Many times, we are so preoccupied with memories of past failures, disappointments, and painful situations that we cannot move forward to where we are supposed to be. This is sad, because we all are created with a purpose. The Lord has given us His Word to take captive every thought and make it obedient to Christ Jesus. Reliving the past can become a terrible stronghold in which the enemy can attack our minds. Then, we are forced to use our valuable time to pull down those strongholds with the Word of God.

We can learn from our past, look at it from God's perspective, and then move forward. I remembered what the Lord said to me: "You cannot change the past; it happened, but My grace is sufficient to help you move past that point and live your life now." Once I came into agreement with the truth of that statement, I was able to move forward. Some of us look back at a moment in time, remembering what we used to have but do not have now. It could be a marriage, a home that was seized through foreclosure, or a car that was repossessed. Whatever it is that keeps us looking back to the past, we need to believe that the Lord has something better for us in the present. He already has our lives planned out according to the blueprint that He has designed. We need to trust Him and look to Him, the author and finisher of our faith (Hebrews 12:2).

Remember that the just shall live by faith and faith is now—not in the past and not in the future. This is our hope. We can change how we are living now by living for Christ and seeking Him first to establish our priorities, allowing His desires to become our desires and believing that they will come to pass. Then, we don't have to let those memories of our past rob our time; instead, we can live by faith now.

Not Having Plans for Our Lives

Not having plans for our lives can also rob us of precious time. We have already seen in the previous chapter how God has plans for our lives to prosper us and give us a future and a hope. We also have noted how effective it is to allow the Lord's plans to direct us through the course of our lives. When we do not have any plans or goals, we aimlessly float through life, either hitting or missing ordained assignments that the Lord has set up for us. Without a well-defined plan, some of us may never reach our destiny or accomplish what the Lord has created us to do.

When we plan a trip, we usually will find out the directions for the shortest route to get to our destination and the travel time involved. If we are traveling by car, we may use a road map or MapQuest on the Internet to find out the best way to travel. If we are flying, we tend to look for a nonstop flight instead of one with connections, since that usually takes more time. Today with our busy schedules, we are very aware that time is a precious commodity. This is why we shouldn't manage our time without first seeking God for the plans that He already has mapped out for our lives.

Some of us believe that it is all right to have our own plans apart from the Lord's insight or wisdom, so we forge ahead with our plans. They proceed along quite nicely until there is a snag. Then, we go to the Lord, wanting to know what went wrong with our plans, instead of facing the truth that we did not ask the Lord for His plans in the first place.

Proverbs 3:5-6 says, "Trust in the Lord with all your heart and lean not on your own understanding. In all your ways acknowledge him, and he will make your paths straight." We should not lean on our own understanding by trying to figure out every minor detail of our lives; instead, we must trust the Lord with all of our heart—not just a part. When we do this, then He will make our paths straight.

We will not have to go down the wrong path, making the wrong decisions about our lives. At school, if we do not learn enough to pass the test to get promoted to the next grade, we are held back to repeat the grade. When we adhere to the principle of this passage, then we will not have to repeat God's life lessons over and over again because we didn't learn them the first time. We don't have to lose any time missing out on the Lord's plans for our lives if we take the time to seek Him first and get His agenda for our days.

Have you ever heard people say that they went to college for four years and graduated but now they do not feel that the career they studied for is what they want to pursue in life? They may have to go back to school to get the degree that they think they want. If they are honest with themselves, they will acknowledge that there may have been times when they did not seek the Lord about His plans for their lives.

Have you ever thought about how your life would have turned out if you had taken the path that was directed by the Lord? Everything that you need to live a prosperous life is on His path—your ministry, financial blessings, marriage, career, relationships, and your business deals. When you trust the Lord with all your heart and allow Him to manage your time the way it is ordained according to His perfect will, then He will make your paths straight to lead you to success—His way.

The Lord's plans are tailor-made to fit the blueprints for our individual lives. God's grace will help us to be who He created us to be—not anyone else. God's plans for our lives will prosper us in every aspect; the plans we devise on our own can never measure up to His. He desires for us to get His plans first before we decide to choose our own plans that will eventually disappoint and even harm us. The good news is that it is never too late to repent from doing our own thing and turn back to the Lord to find out His plans for our lives. It will cost us quality time with Him to receive His wisdom, His strategy, and His instructions on how to live our lives.

The Lord gives us a free will to make good or bad choices. I have decided to submit my will to the Lord's will—not my will, but His will be done. Jesus said that He only did what He saw His Father do in heaven. He carried out the plans that the Father desired for Him to do by submitting His will to do the will of the Father. Jesus had a single-minded focus on what the Father had planned for Him to accomplish, even to the point of dying on the cross to save you and me so that we could have both eternal life and abundant life right now.

You, too, can have a single-minded focus regarding His plans for your life. When you spend time with the Lord, ask Him to show you what things are robbing you of your time and become proactive by getting the Lord's strategy on how to manage your time His way.

Chapter 9

SPIRITUAL DISCIPLINES

Time Management God's Way requires that we practice certain spiritual disciplines to help us grow in our relationship with Christ. When we allow Christ to live His life in and through us, then we will live a spirit-filled life through the power of the Holy Spirit. Spiritual disciplines are Christ-centered practices which help us follow His teachings and grow spiritually by opening ourselves up more fully to God's guidance and His will.

God created us as a trichonomy—we are a spirit housed in a body possessing a soul. Our spirit is designed to grow, just like our bodies. In order for our bodies to grow, we need to feed them physical food for nourishment. We also need to feed our souls with spiritual sustenance from the Word of God.

Studying God's Word

One important spiritual discipline is studying the Word of God so that we will learn more about God, Jesus, the Holy Spirit.

John 1:1 states, "In the beginning was the Word, and the Word was with God, and the Word was God." According to this Scripture, God and His Word (Jesus) are one. John 1:14 states, "And the Word was made flesh, and dwelt among us, (and we beheld his glory, the glory as of the only begotten of the Father,) full of grace and truth" (KJV). This Scripture reveals Jesus to be the "Word made flesh [who] dwelt among us." The Greek translation of "Word" is *logos*, which means the "living word." In essence, Jesus Christ is the manifold wisdom of God and the perfect revelation of the nature and person of God (Ephesians 3:10-11). Jesus Christ is the image of the invisible God, and as the "Word," He reveals the heart and mind of God (Colossians 1:15).

In order for us to understand God's Word, we need to accept Jesus Christ as our Lord and Savior and be born again by receiving His Word in our spirit as an "incorruptible seed by the word of God, which liveth and abideth forever" (1 Peter 1:23). When we receive Christ, we receive the seed of eternal life. The life of God (*zoe*) and His nature are in the seed. God desires to reproduce His nature in us through the incorruptible seed—the Word of God. We are partakers of God's divine nature, so our spirit is joined to God and the Holy Spirit.

Everything that we need to grow spiritually for the purpose that the Lord created us for is in the seed: His Word. God's power, anointing, peace, and joy are already in the seed to help us to grow. When we apply the spiritual discipline of studying the Word of God, we will receive the truth of God's Word in our spirit.

John 17:17 states, "Sanctify them through thy truth; thy word is truth" (KJV). Sanctify means "to make holy, to separate or set apart." Christ prayed to God the Father for His disciples so that they may be sanctified from the world and sin, then set apart to worship and serve God. In John 17:14, Christ told the Father that He gave the disciples the Word of God, but the world hated them because they were not of the world. Christ not only prayed for His disciples but He also prayed for each one of us who are willing to follow Him and be set apart for His use in the kingdom through believing and then obeying the Word.

God's words are spirit and life (John 6:63). The spirit of the word is the Holy Spirit, and the life of God's Word is directly imparted into our spirits.

Hebrews 4:12 states that the "word of God is quick, and powerful, and sharper than any two-edged sword, piercing even to the dividing asunder of soul and spirit, and of the joints and marrow, and is a discerner of the thoughts and intents of the heart" (KJV). The Word of God is quick, meaning "alive and active." It is sharper than a two-edged sword which reveals how powerful, operative, and effectual it is. The Greek word *machaira* describes a sword that cuts from both sides. This sword was light but strong, and it was the best weapon that soldiers used during that time.

This is an awesome description of God's Word: His Word is like a surgeon's knife that is able to penetrate the very core of our spiritual lives. When we submit our spirit to the Holy Spirit, the Spirit of truth, He will guide us into all truth and show us things to come (John 16:13).

Second Timothy 2:15 states, "Study to shew thyself approved unto God, a workman that needeth not to be ashamed, rightly dividing the word of truth" (KJV). As believers, we are required to study the Bible, which is the inspired Word of God called the Scriptures, from Genesis to Revelation. Second Timothy 3:16-17 states, "All Scripture is God-breathed and is useful for teaching, rebuking, correcting and training in righteousness, so that the man of God may be thoroughly equipped for every good work." All Scripture is "God-breathed," a phrase that comes from the Greek word *theopneustos* which is composed of two words: *theos*, meaning "God" and *pneo*, meaning "to breathe." God breathed His holy Word into holy men who then wrote it down by the direction of the Holy Spirit. Scripture is the written Word of God, derived from the Greek word *graphe*, which means graphically stated for us.

Second Peter 1:20-21 assures us that "no prophecy of the Scripture is from any private interpretation," but rather came from holy men of God who spoke as they were moved by the Holy Spirit. "For whatsoever things were written aforetime were written for our learning, that we through patience and comfort of the Scriptures might have hope" (Romans 15:4, KJV). We can receive wisdom from the Old Testament as well as the New Testament regarding living godly lives.

As we continue to study the Word of God, we should long for the pure spiritual milk of the Word until we mature and are able to eat something stronger (Hebrews 5:12-14). We should not be satisfied with just studying the Bible, but we should desire for the Word of God to dwell in us richly (Colossians 3:16). The Word should be in two places: in our heart and in our mouth (Romans 10:8). Jesus told His disciples that "out of the abundance of the heart, the mouth will speak" (Matthew 12:34).

Is your heart filled with the Word of God? Meditation will help us plant the Word of God deep down in our hearts. Then, when danger or life circumstances come against us, we can speak the Word of God out of the abundance of our hearts as the Holy Spirit brings it to our remembrance.

Meditating on the Word of God

Meditating on the Word of God is another spiritual discipline that is important to the life of the believer. The dictionary defines *meditate* as "to engage in contemplation or reflection." It means "to focus your thoughts on, reflect on, or ponder over." Reflection signifies forming an image of an object, and then thinking about it or considering it seriously. "Ponder" refers to weighing or carefully considering thoughts by mulling them over in the mind and in the heart. It is the process of digesting mental food—sowing words and reaping thoughts, as well as sowing thoughts and reaping actions. We should pray for a heart-hunger to eat the Word of God and a subsequent passion to act on it.

Biblical meditation involves the believer mulling over, thinking on, musing upon, and pondering over the Word of God. It is chewing on the Word until it becomes a living reality. Meditation on Scripture is like a cow going through the process of mastication, bringing up previously digested food for renewed grinding and preparation for assimilation. Likewise, mulling over a scriptural passage may be difficult to understand until we are able to digest it and assimilate it into an area of need. Everything that we need is in the Word. The Word of God is a lamp unto our feet and a light unto our path (Psalm 119:105), which will lead us into God's way of prosperity, blessings, and success.

Often we want to manage our lives the world's way, which is not only void of God's Word, but will also steer us down a path of temporary success that only leads to more stress. Meditating on the Word of God, however, will lead us down a path that will give us illumination from its light so that we can see where we are going. Then we will receive revelation that will take us into another dimension of the spiritual realm. Subsequently, we can tap into the creative power of God and His blessings that are available to us so that we can fulfill the Lord's purpose for our lives.

All the instructions on how to live according to the kingdom of God and His righteous standards can be found in the Word of God. The personality behind the Word of God is God Himself, which includes His attributes and character. The Word of God will not only renew our minds, but it will also be established in our hearts and become a part of us as we meditate on its content.

James 1:21 says that the engrafted word is able to save our soul—the mind, will, and emotions. This means that the Word of God should be planted in us and become a part of our very being. God gave us His Word as a good seed to be planted in our hearts so that it will reproduce His life and nature in our lives, specifically to change our character and behavior. The Lord desires that we as His spiritual children have the Word of God abiding in us so that we can become fruitful and abound in every good work that He calls us to do.

God's Word will help us mature spiritually and walk as the Lord did on the earth. Romans 12:2 states, "And be not conformed to this world: but be ye transformed by the renewing of your mind, that ye may prove what is that good, and acceptable, and perfect will of God" (KJV). God's Word will give us specific guidelines to follow. When we submit to the Word of God, then the Holy Spirit can use it to renew, re-educate, and redirect our minds to do the will of God. As our minds are renewed by the Word of God, we will reflect God's character and be transformed into the image of Christ

Meditation is the act of infusing or appropriating the nature of God in our lives. Through meditation, we will learn His will and come into agreement with it for our lives. When we meditate on the Word of God, a prophetic path of victory already pre-planned by God is created. The spirit of the Word will be infused into our human spirit, which will engage the Spirit of truth (the Holy Spirit), who will guide us into all truth and show us things to come (John 16:13). Meditating on biblical passages will activate the Spirit of truth because God's Word *is* truth—and Christ Jesus is the truth. By humbly reflecting on the truth in His Word, the Holy Spirit will direct us how to receive the fulfillment of His promises.

Moreover, we need to have our minds conformed to God's way of thinking because He already has planned for us to live stress-free and prosperous lives. First Corinthians 2:16 states, "For who hath known the mind of the Lord, that he may instruct him? But we have the mind of Christ." Our minds must be renewed in order for us to see things from God's perspective, which entails knowing His will and what He values. The question we should ask ourselves is this—are we spending enough quality time with Christ Jesus and meditating on His Word?

God admonished Joshua and the children of Israel: "Do not let this Book of the Law depart from your mouth; meditate on it day and night, so that you may be careful to do everything written in it. Then you will be prosperous and successful" (Joshua 1:8). This verse applies to every believer as well, for "Whatsoever things were written aforetime were written for our learning" (Romans 15:4, KJV). We should observe and practice what is written in the Word.

Many of us may not be living the prosperous and successful lives that the Lord has ordained for us because we do not take the time to meditate on His Word. Meditation helps us bind the truth to our memory and prepares us to observe and do all that is written in the Word so that we can be prosperous and successful. For me, it's worth it to include quality time in my daily schedule to meditate on the Word of God so that my will can be motivated to conform to His will.

James 1:22 tells us that we must be "doers of the word; not hearers only" (KJV). If we apply this verse to our lives, we will strive to do what the Bible says. After you meditate deeply on the Word, you will be supernaturally energized to obey His words deposited within your spirit.

Psalm 39:3 states, "My heart was hot within me, while I was musing the fire burned: then spake I with my tongue" (KJV). "Muse" means "to meditate." While David was meditating on the Word, he encountered the Spirit behind the words, and it became like fire shut up in his bones. The key to obedience is meditation. The fire of His Word will ignite you to move you from a place of disobedience to obedience. That fire will burn up anything that is not like God and nourish our spirit at the same time.

Meditation also involves memorizing Scriptures; it is like recycling the Word from the inside out. The Word enters your spirit, and then you hear yourself say it as it comes back into your being. Now, the Word is being established within your heart. Colossians 3:16 exhorts us to let the Word of Christ dwell in us richly in all wisdom; therefore, we can confess what is already established inside of us. We need to meditate on the Word for it to be grounded within us. Then we can expect success to come to us because we have sowed the Word in our heart and will eventually reap the blessings.

Psalms 1:1-3 tells us that when we meditate on the Word of God day and night, we will be like a tree planted by the rivers of water, allowing us to bring forth fruit in its season and prosper along the way. The psalmist is telling us that we can learn how to follow God and His moral standards by meditating on His Word. We need to set time aside in our busy lives to read, think, and ponder on God's Word so that we can obey what it says. Then, we can apply the Word to every area of our lives. The more we understand the Word of God, the more revelation we will receive to know God and His ways. The decisions we make throughout the course of our lives should be governed by the Word of God operating in us. Then we will be like trees soaking up God's Word which will produce actions and attitudes that honor Him.

Meditating on the Word of God will help us hide the Word in our hearts so that we will not sin against God (Psalm 119:11). Memorizing Scripture, meditating on the Word, and submitting to God will help us overcome worry, doubt, fear, and unbelief. Allowing His promises to be written in our minds will cause us to experience His perfect peace that will guard our hearts. We will experience immediate benefits and become better equipped to meet future needs and opportunities.

First Timothy 4:15 states, "Meditate upon these things; give thyself wholly to them; that thy profiting may appear to all" (KJV). When we meditate on the Word of God, then we will be able to think on those things that are true, honest, pure, lovely, and of a good report (Philippians 4:8), which will in turn allow us to fix our minds on those things that bring us peace and freedom from anxiety. Will we take the time to meditate on Matthew 6:33? "Seek first the kingdom of God and His righteousness and all these things shall be added unto you."

Time Management God's Way requires us to put God and His Word first in our lives so that we may observe and do what is required of us. "Observe" implies that we are able to see the end from the beginning, which the Holy Spirit will show us how to do. With our new "faith eyes," we will be able to see beyond the present into the future. The eyes of our human spirit will be illuminated by the light of the Word of God to receive and enjoy a prophetic path of blessings that He has created for us. Then we won't have to try to find our way in the dark, because we have begun to walk in the light. The Lord desires for us to walk by faith and not by sight.

The Lord placed on my heart that some of us do not have the Word established within our souls. He asked me this question: "Who would drive their car at night in the dark with their headlights dim?" I told Him that I wouldn't do that because I couldn't see and might hit something by accident. The Lord said that many of His children have their spiritual lights dim, so they are bumping around in the dark, trying to find the direction they should go.

I needed to repent because I hadn't heeded Joshua 1:8 by making time to meditate on the Word, memorize it, and submit to it so that it could be established in my soul. From then on, when the enemy, circumstances, challenges, or trials came, the Holy Spirit would bring relevant verses from the Word of God to my remembrance. Then I could proactively respond like Jesus during His time of temptation in the wilderness: "It is written."

Exercising Our Faith

Another spiritual discipline is "call[ing] those things that are not as though they were" (Romans 4:17). God called Abraham "the father of many nations" before he had any children. Abraham, a man of great faith, came into agreement with what God said about him. Romans 4:20-21 says that Abraham did not stagger at the promise of God through unbelief; but he was strong in faith, giving glory to God; and being fully persuaded that, what he had promised, he was also able to perform it. Likewise, the Lord desires for us to operate in the same way because all His promises are "yes" and "amen" in Christ Jesus (2 Corinthians 1:20).

We need to have the Word of God in two places—in our heart and in our mouth. Matthew 12:34 tells us that out of the abundance of the heart the mouth will speak. When fear tries to grip me, for example, I declare that God did not give me "a spirit of fear but of love, power and a sound mind" and I choose to walk according to the Word (2 Timothy 1:7, KJV). I had to meditate on that verse until it became a part of my very being, because the enemy had been attacking me with fear and it was affecting me in every area of my life.

Fear can be so paralyzing that you cannot do what you already know how to do. After meditating on 2 Timothy 1:7, I knew without a shadow of doubt that God had not given me a spirit of fear. If it did not come from Him, then it had to come from Satan. The Lord assured me that no one had the power to snatch me out of His hand or determine whether I went to heaven or hell.

Once I received the revelation that God was more powerful than the enemy or fear and I came into agreement with the Word, allowing it to be the final authority in my life, I was able to stand in the power and might of the Lord and boldly declare that no weapon (of fear, poverty, sickness, or disease) formed against me would prosper (Isaiah 54:17). By meditating on the Word of God, I was able to have the Word in two places: in my heart and in my mouth. Then, out of the overflow, I was able to speak what was already established in my heart.

As believers, we need to agree with the Word of God, not with what the enemy or circumstances are trying to dictate to us. They may be facts, but these are subject to change by the Word of God. Fortunately for us, however, the truth of God's Word is not subject to change. Thus, when Satan tells us his "facts" of sickness, poverty, negative reports, or anything contrary to the Bible, we can use the Word of God to change the "facts" for two reasons: (1) the Word is eternal, and every circumstance is temporal; and (2) God and His Word are one. Not only did He create the world with His Word but He sustains the world with His Word.

When people say that I am in denial regarding the facts, I let them know that I have made a quality decision to come into agreement with what the Word says. I am not denying the facts, but I choose to respond in faith, believing the Word and allowing it to have the final authority in my life. I want to respond like Abraham in Romans 4:17-21. Even though the facts said that he was a hundred years old and Sarah's womb was dead, he still came into agreement with what God had said about him. The Word has the authority and power to back up what it intends to carry out.

Luke 4:36 tells us that when Jesus spoke the word to drive out unclean spirits, His word has authority and power. As believers, we too have the authority to speak the Word of God with power and expect the Lord to watch over His Word to perform it. We can call those things that are not as though they were according to the Word of God because the Lord said that it will not return to Him void, but it shall accomplish that which pleases Him, and it will prosper in the area that He sent it to (Isaiah 55:10-11, KJV). Second Corinthians 4:13 states, "It is written: 'I believed; therefore I have spoken.' With that same spirit of faith we also believe and therefore speak." We must speak and act on what we believe as a demonstration of the spirit of faith operating in us.

Exercising our faith is a spiritual discipline we must cultivate. Biblical faith is defined in Hebrews 11:1. "Now faith is the substance of things hoped for, the evidence of things not seen" (KJV). Faith is now; it is a present reality of things unseen. In other words, faith says that I have received the blessing now, even when I do not see it right away. Faith is solid truth, according to the Word of God. John 17:17 says that God's Word is truth.

The Amplified Bible translates Hebrew 11:1: "Now faith is the assurance (the confirmation, the title deed) of the things [we] hope for, being the proof of things [we] do not see and the conviction of their reality [faith perceiving as real fact what is not revealed to the senses]." Faith is the evidence or proof that you have what has been promised; therefore, you don't need to see it to believe it. For example, if someone told you that you own a house and you hold the title deed, you don't need to see the house to believe it because you have the title deed.

Believers need to live more in the evidence than in the manifestation. We have things not because we see them first; we have them because they are reserved for us in the bank of heaven. Romans 12:3 (KJV) says that God has dealt every man a measure of faith. Are we using the faith He has given us?

The source of faith is the Word of God. You can receive faith from the *rhema*, the revealed word of God; from the *graphe*, the written word graphically stated in the Bible; or from the *logos*, the living Word who is alive and active to work in us—Jesus.

Jesus is the living Word, as well as the author and finisher of our faith (Hebrews 12:2). It is important for the Word of God to dwell richly within us in order to feed our faith. We need to ingest a continuous diet of the Word of God so that we can have confidence that what God says will come to pass. We must speak the Word of God for our faith to operate at its fullest potential, because whatever we speak in faith can happen.

Romans 10:8 tells us that the word of faith is near us; it is in our mouth and in our heart. It comes by what we hear according to Romans 10:17; therefore, we need to take time to listen to faith-filled words that will build up our faith. When we get saved, we have confessed with our mouths, "Jesus is Lord," and believed in our hearts that God has raised Him from the dead. At some point, we heard the gospel preached, which is "the power of God for the salvation of everyone who believes" (Romans 1:16).

There are two types of faith: positive and negative. Both develop from what we hear and believe. As believers, we have the God-kind of faith in which we put our complete confidence in God and His Word.

God desires for each one of us to walk by faith and not by sight. We can only do this if we are abiding in His Word and allowing it to light up the path that we should walk on. Many times, I have walked down the wrong path because I did not allow God's Word to guide me and instruct me in the way that I should go. The Lord desires for us to manage our time in such a way that we can walk down the straight and narrow path that leads to victory instead of disappointment, defeat, and deception.

With God, all things are possible to them who believe (Mark 9:23). Faith has a corresponding action that agrees with God and His Word. On the other hand, we cannot speak in faith and allow our actions to say something else.

This reminds me of the time I received a *rhema* word from the Lord regarding a debt-free car. Once I came into agreement with that word, I immersed myself into studying the Word of God to build up my faith because I could not see how it would happen. Faith told me that I had the debt-free car now, even before it materialized, and hope said that it would come to pass. The Lord impressed upon my heart to clean out my car that was not working well as an act of faith so He could bless me with another car that was debt-free.

I made the mistake of telling some people that I was believing God for a debt-free car because they began to speak words of doubt and unbelief. I learned the valuable lesson of not sharing what the Lord had spoken to me with those who do not operate with the God-kind of faith. Amos 3:3 says, "Can two walk together, except they be agreed?" (KJV).

I asked the Lord to bring believers across my path to accompany me on my faith walk, and He did.

I began to walk by faith, not by what I saw or perceived with my five senses. My head knowledge was trying to figure out how God was going to work it out. I was responsible for my part, which was to trust God and believe what He said. I just had to exercise my faith according to the power of God that was working in me for what I was hoping for. I kept a picture in my mind of a debt-free car that would become reality because of my faith.

I had to allow patience to develop my faith so that I would not move from the place of receiving my blessing from God before it materialized. Faith and patience will help you realize your dream or promise.

Hebrews 6:12 tells us not to be slothful, but to be followers of them who through faith and patience inherited the promises, just like Abraham who had patiently endured; then he received the promise of his son (Hebrews 6:15). God is not a man that He should lie (Numbers 23:19, Hebrews 6:18). It is up to us to trust Him and wait for His perfect timing to bring about the manifestation of the promise.

I did wait patiently for the visible manifestation of God's promise to me, and it was fulfilled. While I was waiting, however, trials and tribulations came my way to try my faith. I discovered that patience is worked out in the crucible of life. James 1:3 says that the trying of our faith will work patience. I decided not to be unwavering in my faith walk, but to come into agreement with whatever the Lord spoke to me. Because I knew that the Lord loved me, I knew that He would not dangle this promise before me to "mess with my head" because He had already spoken to my spirit that His character does not allow Him to do that. This reassurance helped me to patiently wait for His timing. What if I had not known His character? Could I have stood the test? The Lord was trying to stretch my faith to believe for the impossible.

The Lord placed it on a believer's heart to bless me with cash to purchase a debt-free car. When I received this debt-free car, my faith increased another level. My daughters named the car "Faith." This was a great opportunity to share my faith with my daughters, family, friends, and others when I was led by the Holy Spirit.

Once I received this basic principle of faith, I chose as an act of my will to put my faith in action by coming into agreement with the Word of God. If God said it, that settled it for me. Now, I look for every opportunity to use my faith. I allow my spirit to engage the Spirit of truth, who will reveal the truth to me pertaining to the Word that I am acting on. I told the Lord that I don't want to get anything without exercising my faith first. I know that may sound radical, but that is where I am right now in my faith walk. The Lord is looking for someone who looks to and responds like Him. He made us in His image to take dominion over all that He shows us so that people will see our good works and give Him the glory.

It is impossible to please the Lord without faith, and we have to believe that He is a *rewarder* of those who diligently seek Him (Hebrews 11:6). We cannot come to Him in prayer without believing that we'll receive what we ask of Him before we receive it.

In Mark 11:22-24, Jesus answered the disciples, "Have faith in God. I tell you the truth, if anyone says to this mountain, 'Go, throw yourself in the sea,' and does not doubt in his heart but believes that what he says will happen, it will be done for him. Therefore I tell you, whatever you ask for in prayer, believe that you received it, and it will be yours."

Prayer

Another spiritual discipline that is vital to our Christian walk is prayer. Prayer is a dialogue, not a monologue. Some people think that there is only one aspect of praying to God—to have a nonstop talk with Him. Yet, the Lord also desires to speak to us and tell us some things that are on His heart. Do we take time to listen to what God has to say? This is an important question to consider for doing time management God's way, because it requires that we make time to seek Him to see what He has to say about our lives, our vision, our mission, our family, our ministry, our deliverance from habits, and sin in our lives. There is so much that the Lord desires to share with us, but it will cost us our busyness with all of life's ins and outs. Matthew 6:33 tells us to seek first God's kingdom and His righteousness and all that we need will be added to us. When we seek God, we also should seek His Word to guide us in our time of prayer.

Once we have the Word abiding in us, we can make a request of the Father in the name of Jesus, and it will be given to us (John 15:16). John 16:23-24 states, "In that day you will no longer ask me anything. I tell you the truth, my Father will give you whatever you ask in my name. Until now you have not asked for anything in my name. Ask and you will receive, and your joy will be complete."

All of our petitions should be addressed to God the Father, not to Jesus. God is the Father in heaven, the Creator of heaven and earth, and the Father of the Lord Jesus who is the Savior of all mankind. God will only accept the sacrifice that Jesus offers: Himself. Jesus is now in heaven making intercession for each one of us. God has prepared a way for us to come boldly to the throne of grace in time of need and make our petitions known to Him through His Son Jesus, our high priest who made us acceptable with Him (Hebrews 4:16).

It is important for us to pray according to God's will for our lives in order for our prayers to be answered. First John 5:14-15 states, "This is the confidence we have in approaching God: that if we ask anything according to his will, he hears us. And if we know that he hears us—whatever we ask—we know that we have what we asked of him."

When we ask God the Father, in the name of Jesus, according to the will of God, then we will receive what we asked for. God's Word is His will, and Jesus is the Word (John 1:1, 14), so whatever we ask according to Jesus (the Word), the Father will give to us.

For prayer to be effective in our lives, we need to spend time getting the Word in our hearts so that our prayers will be Word-based. Then, we will not "pray the problem" but we will "pray the promises of God." The Lord will watch over His Word to perform it (Jeremiah 1:12), but not negative words. Prayer is speaking the Word of God which takes dominion over things that are contrary to the will of God.

Our motives have to be right to move us into a place of desiring what is good for the kingdom of God and His purposes for our lives. James 4:3 says that when we ask with wrong motives or wrong reasons, we do not receive from the Lord because we wanted those things to spend on our pleasures. When we spend time in the Word of God, however, we will be full of His Word. Out of the abundance of our hearts, we will say prayers that are not selfish but ones that will honor Him and His purposes. When we make spending time with Him and His Word our top priority, we will be able to trust Him to meet all our needs because He already knows what we need.

Philippians 2:13 tells us that it is God who works in us both to will and to do His good pleasure. *Time Management God's Way* is being willing to do His will instead of our own. It is awesome how I am more open to do God's will when I take the time to get quiet and stay in His presence—just to spend some quality time with Him. Yes, I have to push aside the distractions of everyday life to get alone with Him during my prayer time, but it is worth it when I can hear His small, still voice and sense His presence, for then I know that He is near me. It reminds me of Jesus' prayer life: He would always get alone with God to spend quality time with Him.

In John 5:19, Jesus tells us that He can do nothing of Himself, but only what he sees the Father do. In order for Jesus to focus that intently on what the Father does, He has to stay in very close fellowship with Him which is true intimacy.

Prayer is intimacy with God, and Jesus modeled this kind of relationship with the Father for us.

Prayer comes from the Greek word *proseuche*, meaning communion with God or "common-union"—spirit-to-Spirit communication in which we are sharing with one another. The quality of our prayer life determines the quality of our relationship with Him. How much time do you spend in prayer with God? Do you spend time preparing your heart for fellowship with God?

Fellowship comes from the Greek word *koinonia*, which literally means "having in common;" it also involves sharing and participation. When I think of fellowship according to this description, it helps me to see what I have in common with God.

God, Jesus, and His Word are all one; therefore, I need to share and participate with all three.

It is important to study, meditate, and memorize the Word of God because we need to be in constant agreement with the Word. Also, God is holy; without holiness no one will see God (Hebrews 12:14). Thus, we need the Word to cleanse and wash us, as well as the blood of Jesus to purify us from all unrighteousness so that we can be in right standing with God. God is light, and in Him there is no darkness (1 John 1:5). This means that I need to walk in the light of the truth of His Word as I apply it to my life in order for me to experience intimate fellowship with the Lord.

When we abide in Christ and let His words abide in us, then we will share His life by the indwelling Spirit living in us. The more we stay connected to Christ through meditation on the Word, the more our prayers will line up with His nature and His Word. When we partake of His divine nature and life, we begin to experience revelation knowledge about the Father, Son, and Holy Spirit and develop closer fellowship with them.

Holy Spirit Baptism

The apostle Paul considered praying in tongues to be an important spiritual discipline in the life of the believer. First Corinthians 14:14-15 says, "For if I pray in an unknown tongue, my spirit prayeth, but my understanding is unfruitful. What is it then? I will pray with the spirit, and I will pray with the understanding also: I will sing with the spirit, and I will sing with the understanding also" (KJV). When I pray in tongues, my spirit prays as the Holy Spirit gives utterance.

The word "tongues," derived from the Greek word *glossa*, which means language, is considered one of the God-given signs accompanying the baptism of the Holy Spirit. When speaking in tongues, the born-again believer is uttering what the Holy Spirit is placing in their spirit by faith. Mark 16:17 says that signs will accompany those who believe in Christ Jesus, and speaking in tongue is one of them.

First Corinthians 14:2 says, "For he that speaketh in an unknown tongue speaketh not unto men, but unto God: for no man understandeth him; howbeit in the spirit he speaketh mysteries" (KJV). The Greek word for "mystery" in this context is *musterion*, which is a sacred thing that is naturally unknown by human reasoning, but is only known by the revelation of God. By saying things that are not understandable to himself or the hearer, the believer can pray to God about divine secrets or mysteries. Tongues also allow him to pray for God's perfect will because the communication is spirit-to-Spirit, which is void of error.

The apostle Paul made this clear in 1 Corinthians 4:1: "Let a man so account of us, as of the ministers of Christ, and stewards of the mysteries of God" (KJV). We call these sacred things mysteries because we don't have any natural understanding of them, but we have the spiritual understanding because it is a spiritual language which the Holy Spirit has taught our spirit. First Corinthians 2:12-14 says, "Now we have received, not the spirit of the world, but the spirit which is of God; that we might know the things that are freely given to us of God. Which things also we speak, not in the words which man's wisdom teacheth, but which the Holy Ghost teacheth; comparing spiritual things with spiritual. But the natural man receiveth not the things of the Spirit of God: for they are foolishness unto him: neither can he know them, because they are spiritually discerned" (KJV).

When you pray in tongues, you are building yourself up in the most holy faith (Jude 20).You are speaking utterances directed by the Holy Spirit as you commune with God in the form of prayer, praise, singing, blessing, thanksgiving, or taking authority over Satan. Mark 16:17 states, "And these signs shall follow them that believe; in my name shall they cast out devils; they shall speak with new tongues" (KJV).

On the day of Pentecost, the 120 believers were gathered in the upper room, all in one accord. Acts 2:3-4 states, "They saw what seemed to be tongues of fire that separated and came to rest on each of them. All of them were filled with the Holy Spirit and began to speak in other tongues as the Spirit enabled them." The "other tongues" referred to in this story were existing languages on earth they had not learned. In Acts 2:5-6, when a crowd came together and heard the disciples speaking in other tongues, they were bewildered because each one heard them speaking in his own language so they could be understood.

Tongues also can refer to languages unknown on earth, described in 1 Corinthians 13:1 as "tongues of angels." Speaking in tongues, or receiving a heavenly prayer language, is one of the outward signs of the baptism of the Holy Spirit. Acts 1:4b-5 says, "Do not leave Jerusalem, but wait for the gift my Father promised, which you have heard me speak about. For John baptized with water, but in a few days you will be baptized with the Holy Spirit."

The preposition "with" in Acts 1:5 comes from the Greek word *en*, which means "in." "Baptized *with* the Holy Spirit" is usually translated as "baptized *in* the Holy Spirit." The gift that the Father promised is the baptism in the Holy Spirit. Once you are saved and baptized into the body of Christ, then you can receive the power of the Holy Spirit to effectively witness for Christ in proclaiming the gospel of Christ throughout the world (Acts 1:8). 1 Corinthians 12:13 says, "For we were all baptized by one Spirit into one body—whether Jews or Greeks, slave or free—and we all were given the one Spirit to drink." John 4:14 says, "But whoever drinks the water I give him will never thirst. Indeed, the water I give him will become in him a spring of water welling up to eternal life."

Jesus is speaking about the born-again believer drinking from the living water: Jesus Christ Himself. After receiving the baptism of the Holy Spirit, he experiences an infilling of the Spirit's power that are streams of living water flowing from within him. John 7:38-39 says, "'Whoever believes in me, as the Scripture has said, streams of living water will flow from within him.' By this he meant the Spirit, whom those who believed in Him were later to receive."

Moreover, Acts 2:38 states, "Then Peter said unto them, Repent, and be baptized, every one of you in the name of Jesus Christ for the remission of sins, and ye shall receive the gift of the Holy Ghost" (KJV). The aforementioned Scriptures clearly show that one has to believe in Jesus to be born again and later receive the baptism in the Spirit.

When we are filled with the Spirit, we will be empowered to carry out the mission of Christ to be witnesses for Him through works of service as directed by the leading of the Holy Spirit. This infilling is not a one-time event but should be a continuous infilling or refreshing that allows the rivers of living water to flow from our innermost being to quench the parched areas in our lives and for all who come across our path.

One may ask, "How can I receive the baptism in the Holy Spirit?" Once you repent and turn from the kingdom of darkness to the kingdom of light and receive Jesus as your Lord and Savior, all you have to do is ask Jesus to baptize you in the Spirit, receive it by faith and then thank Him for it.

Luke 11:13 shows us that the Father in heaven will give the Holy Spirit to those who ask Him. For those who are not sure if they have received the baptism in the Holy Spirit, the question is, "Have you received the baptism in the Holy Spirit since you believed in Christ?"

In Acts 19:2, the apostle Paul asks the same question to the Ephesian disciples. Their answer was, "No, we have not even heard that there is a Holy Spirit." Paul then explained to them that the baptism of John was one of repentance they had received at the time of conversion when they were born again by the Spirit into the body of Christ. He informed them that the baptism in the Holy Spirit is a separate and unique experience from salvation. In verses 5 and 6, the disciples heard what the apostle Paul said concerning the baptism in the Spirit, so they were baptized into the name of Jesus. After Paul baptized them in water and laid hands on them, the Holy Spirit came on them, and they spoke in tongues.

Simply stated, upon conversion as a born-again believer, you automatically receive the indwelling presence of the Holy Spirit. Now that you believe in Christ, you can also receive the *fullness* of the Spirit when you ask for the baptism in the Spirit by faith; then, He will fill you with His power to be witnesses for Him.

Satan will try to bring confusion among us by deceiving us into thinking that we do not need the baptism in the Holy Spirit. If he cannot stop us from being born again, then he will try to stop us from receiving the Spirit's power.

If you are a believer and have not yet received the baptism of the Spirit, ask your Father in heaven, and He will grant you this free gift. By faith, begin to speak as the Spirit gives you utterance. Open your mouth and begin to praise God for what He has done for you. Don't try to mentally figure out what is going on; just speak by faith whatever the Spirit enables you. This is not a mental exercise, but a spiritual experience that will build you up from the inside out.

For those of you who already speak in tongues, continue to practice this important discipline, edifying your spirit man and speaking mysteries unto God. Speaking in tongues helps you to be very sensitive to the Spirit's promptings and presence. Jesus said that the Spirit would lead and guide us into all truth and show us things to come: "I have much more to say to you, more than you can now bear. But when he, the Spirit of truth, comes, he will guide you into all truth. He will not speak on his own; he will speak only what he hears, and he will tell you what is yet to come. He will bring glory to me by taking from what is mine and making it known to you" (John 6:12-14).

Because the Holy Spirit knows the mind of Christ, He will make it known to us. Why not stir up the gift inside you and pray in tongues to help you to be sensitive to the Holy Spirit—to hear what He has to say and to see what is yet to come?

Fasting

Another discipline for us to practice is fasting. The word "fast" comes from the Hebrew word *tsum*, which means "to cover your mouth." The Greek word for "fast" is *nesteuo*, meaning "to abstain from food." Fasting is a discipline that the Lord is calling us to develop in order to become more sensitive to hear His voice. Fasting helps us to focus on God and seek His kingdom first as Jesus commands us to do in Matthew 6:33.

Denying yourself food to center on God, His kingdom, and His righteousness will put you in a place of humility. Psalms 35:13 says, "But as for me, when they were sick, my clothing was sackcloth: I humbled my soul with fasting; and my prayer returned into mine own bosom" (KJV). Spiritually, fasting is a humbling experience of worship that shows great honor and respect for God and His kingdom values. It involves turning away from our desires and surrendering to God's way through deep communion.

Some people confuse a physical fast with a spiritual fast. The Hebrew and Greek words for "fast" define that a "spiritual (biblical) fast" is first and foremost the abstaining from food to focus on God who is Spirit. The spiritual fast is one that is directed by the Holy Spirit to lead us to a place of worshipping the Lord to help us discern His plans for our lives—whether it be goals, vision, provision, assignments, deliverance, or intercession for someone else. Seeking the Lord through fasting will also help us discern good from evil to keep us from falling for the same temptations that Satan places before us day after day.

A physical fast primarily means to abstain from food for a period of time for health benefits, not necessarily spiritual benefits or direction from the Lord. During a fast, the body will get rid of unneeded toxins, which will improve the health of the blood, heart, and other parts of the body. In short, the main difference between a physical fast and a spiritual fast is focus. With a physical fast, the focus is on the body's health; with a spiritual fast, the focus is on becoming spiritually attuned to the Spirit of God for direction in some area of life.

Some people say that we can fast from reading books and magazines, or watching TV, but that is not a true biblical fast. According to the Greek words, *tsum* and *nesteuo*, fasting means to "cover your mouth and to abstain from food," not daily activities. Personally, however, during a biblical fast I will also refrain from doing those things in my normal daily routine to devote myself to studying and meditating on the Word of God, as well as seeking the Lord in prayer.

During my quiet time with the Lord, I will silence every voice that tries to compete with the voice of God, including unnecessary mental chatter that attempts to distract me from hearing the voice of God. Also, I silence the voice of Satan and take captive every thought that exalts itself higher than the knowledge of God and make it obedient to our Lord Jesus Christ (2 Corinthians 10:5).

Silencing these distracting voices will help to keep your focus on seeking God and His righteousness during your time of fasting. The flesh, desiring to satisfy its appetites and desires, will war with your spirit that wants to worship the Lord and commune with Him. When you submit to this discipline of spiritual fasting, your spirit will override the flesh and subsequently be more willing to be led by the Holy Spirit who will guide you into all truth. You must always let your spirit control you instead of the flesh.

In 1 Corinthians 9:27, the apostle Paul says that he keeps his body under, and brings it into, subjection. We need to discipline ourselves by bringing our body into submission to our spirit and developing self-control to walk after the Spirit and not after the flesh.

According to Galatians 5:16, God desires for us to manage our time in such a way that we walk in the Spirit, so that we will not fulfill the lust of the flesh. When we walk in the Spirit, we are walking in love; that is, we are living a lifestyle of love. Since God is love, according to 1 John 4:8, then we who dwell in love abide in God. The manifestation of this love is illustrated in Galatians 5:22-23 that lists the fruit of the Spirit.

Developing a lifestyle of fasting will help us to control our desires and be more sensitive to the promptings and guidance of the Holy Spirit. Remember that the spirit is willing to submit to the Holy Spirit, but the flesh is weak. When we fast, our spirit will override our bodies' cravings and, as a result, be more in tune with the Holy Spirit. The Spirit will convict us of any sin in our lives by making us aware of God's righteousness and then call us to a place of repentance. It is our responsibility to be Spirit-led and the Holy Spirit's responsibility to teach, correct, and guide us into all truth (John 16:13). When we are led by the Spirit of God, then we are the sons of God (Romans 8:14).

We should check our motives for fasting because we do not want hypocrisy or pride creeping in to distract our focus. Our motivation to fast should be out of our love for God and His kingdom, along with our love and genuine concern for others. This is the kind of fast that God has chosen for every born-again believer: to fast as unto to Him, which pleases Him.

Isaiah 58:6 states, "Is not this the fast that I have chosen? to loose the bands of wickedness, to undo the heavy burdens, and to let the oppressed go free, and that ye break every yoke?" (KJV). God desires us to fast with humble spirits and a heart that is willing to seek Him completely. Then, we will be in tune with the heartbeat of God, seeking to obey His commands and meet the needs of those who are physically, emotionally, and financially in need.

Fasting and prayer will also empower our faith by enabling the Word of God to be effective in a specific area of concern. In Matthew 17:14-21, the disciples realized that they could not cast the demons out of a boy, but Jesus could. Jesus said that this kind of demon only comes out through prayer and fasting. Sometimes, our prayers need an extra boost that can only be supplied by fasting, especially to destroy the power of oppression through deliverance, so that those who are bound can be set free.

One may ask, "When should a Christian fast?" My response would be, "When you sense the Spirit of God leading you to fast." The fast may be prompted by a spiritual concern or issue that you are going through at the time. The Holy Spirit may be leading you to fast on behalf of someone else or to help someone get delivered and set free from demonic bondage.

There are several Scriptures that describe the length of the fast, but we should seek the Lord to see what He is calling us individually to do. Judges 20:26 and 2 Samuel 1:12 give examples of a "normal fast," which was usually for one day. The length of the Jewish day was from sunset to sunset, so this meant that the fast would be broken after sundown. To intercede on behalf of Israel's deliverance, Queen Esther called for an extended fast of abstaining from food or drink for three days and nights (Esther 5:16).

In 2 Samuel 12:16-18, David fasted seven days for his child who was very sick. The Scriptures say that David didn't eat, but not that he didn't drink water. We need to be careful not to put ourselves in harm's way by fasting without water for more than one day, which is considered a normal fast. We should check with our doctors or pastors if we are not sure how we should fast. If we have health problems or take medicine, we should definitely check with the doctor. Remember that we aren't fasting as a ritual but as a lifestyle that is disciplined through our obedience to God, His Word, and the promptings of His Spirit.

In Summary

All these spiritual disciplines are important practices for the normal life of the believer. Studying, meditating on, and praying the Word of God will give us spiritual insight for our life journey by illuminating our way and helping us navigate through a dark and perverse world. Without the light of God's Word, it will prove difficult to see with our faith eyes to obtain success according to

God's kingdom principles and plans for our lives. When we know the Word of God, then we can receive revelation of who God is and who we are in Christ Jesus, the living Word.

When I submit myself to these disciplines, I become sensitive to God's voice, His presence, and His prodding. We do not know what the Lord will speak to our spirit that can change our lives forever. The Lord desires for us to redeem the time because the days are evil (Ephesians 5:16). We need to be careful how we live our lives, not as the unwise but as the wise, making the most of every opportunity that the Lord gives us.

God gave us His Word, His Spirit, and spiritual disciplines to help us to grow spiritually in Christ Jesus and in our relationship with God. He also gave each of us enough time to carry out the plan He created for us. The question is, "Are you managing your time to do what God created you to do?" If you are not managing your time according to the principles of *Time Management God's Way*, it is not too late to pray and ask God to help you release your time into His hands and trust Him as your time manager.

Chapter 10

PRACTICAL APPLICATION: MAKING TIME FOR GOD AND HIS WORD

I have applied the principles of *Time Management's God's Way* and found them to be beneficial for every aspect of my life. When I trust God to be my time manager, I am not stressed by trying to do everything or please everybody. Instead, I make it a priority to set aside time every day to develop an intimate relationship with Jesus by spending time with Him and studying His Word. I also look for opportunities to be sensitive to the Holy Spirit's voice, His presence, His promptings, and His guidance.

When we acknowledge that God is the giver of time and the authority on how we should manage our time according to His kingdom values and foreordained standards, then we can stop striving after the things of the world. Instead, if we seek God and His kingdom we can change the world! *Time Management God's Way* is based on the biblical principles of sowing and reaping. We sow our time into God's kingdom and then reap a harvest of bountiful blessings from His kingdom, which includes a stress-free and prosperous life.

Once I determined that my top priority was seeking God's counsel, wisdom, plans, and kingdom living for my life, I set aside time to commune with the Lord daily. That time included reading or studying His Word to learn

His voice. Remember that God and His Word are one. You will get to know His character, His ways, His promises, His nature, and His plans for your life through His Word. Often, I don't have time to open up the Word of God, so I talk to the Lord throughout the day about a Scripture that is on my heart. I'll ask Him to give me a fresh revelation from the light of His Word so I can allow that verse to renew my mind throughout the day.

We cannot know God intimately without knowing the Word of God: the *Logos*, or the living Word. Jesus Christ is the Word, as well as the way, the truth, and the life (John 14:6). We need to maintain a steady diet of the Word of God, immersing ourselves through reading, memorizing, and meditating on passages of Scripture.

The Lord also put on my heart to look for opportunities to use the Word or be a doer of the Word and not a hearer only. I cannot tell you how many times the Lord has brought people across my path who needed to hear a word from God. I often asked the Lord to give me an opportunity to sow His Word into the life of someone who needed to hear it. The person who received the word was blessed, and so was I, because I was sowing seeds into God's kingdom. Many times we think that it will be difficult to apply the biblical principles of God's Word to our lives, but it really isn't. God will meet each one of us where we are in our faith walk.

I started mine just by spending time with the Lord and His Word to see what He had to say to me. Often, the Lord would place Scriptures on my heart such as, "Without faith it is impossible to please Me;" and "Faith comes by hearing and hearing by the word of God" (Hebrews 11:6 and Romans 10:17). These two Scriptures are very dear to me because they deal with faith. When I began to seek God, I realized that I had to seek His Word first in my life. The more I read and studied God's Word, the more I developed a passion for it. When the Lord gave me those two Scriptures, I looked them up, memorized them, and later began to meditate on them.

Hebrews 11:5-6 says, "By faith Enoch was translated that he should not see death; and was not found, because God had translated him: for before his translation he had this testimony, that he pleased God. But without faith it is impossible to please him: for he that cometh to God must believe that he is, and that he is a rewarder of them that diligently seek him" (KJV). I realized from meditating on this Scripture that faith was needed to seek God, and that it was impossible for me to please God without it. That settled the issue about whether I needed to use my faith; now I had to find out how to get this faith.

The Holy Spirit directed me to look up Scriptures on faith. I found out that each person has been given a measure of faith (Romans 12:3), but it is up to each of us to exercise our faith. Since faith comes from hearing, and hearing by the Word of God, we need to allow it to renew our minds so that we begin to think like God and develop the God-kind of faith.

We also need the Word to get into our hearts so it will come out of our mouths because out of the abundance of our hearts is what we will speak. If faith is in our hearts, then we will speak faith, but if fear, unbelief, or anything that is contrary to the Word of God is in our hearts, that is what we will speak. In other words, what is inside of us will come out. Now, I am getting excited because I made a quality decision to make God's Word a priority in my life, which in turn allows God Himself to become a priority in my life.

I also desired to be like Enoch in his faith walk. Hebrews 11:5 says that Enoch's faith pleased God so much that He took him up into eternity to be with Him. I decided to make time for studying and meditating on God's Word so that it would feed my faith; now, I have to put my faith to work because faith without works is dead (James 2:17). I began by asking the Lord to give me opportunities to use my faith. The Lord reminded me of Hebrews 11:6, which says that we must first believe that He is, and second, that He is a rewarder of those who diligently seek Him.

We must believe that God is whomever we need Him to be, based on His promises found throughout the Bible. There are times when I need God to be my healer, deliverer, provider, etc., depending on my circumstances. The question I have to ask myself is, "Do I know which Scripture pertains to a particular promise, and do I believe that God will watch over His word to perform it?

Hebrews 6:18 says that it is impossible for God to lie. It is up to us to believe what the Word of God says; if we do not believe, we will not receive from the Lord. Also, the Lord reminded me that I must believe that He is a rewarder of those who diligently seek Him. This has changed my mindset when I come before the Lord; I now have a spirit of expectancy to receive whatever the Lord desires for me to have. I must believe that I have received the blessing before it appears. Faith says that I have it now. Can you see how the Lord was ordering my steps through this scriptural passage? It is not enough just to read the Word of God. We must want the Holy Spirit to teach us the truth of God's Word as well. Then, we will be given opportunities to apply the biblical, eternal truths to every aspect of our being for an overall positive effect on our lives.

Time Management God's Way requires us to be proactive in setting aside time to meditate on God's Word and allowing the Holy Spirit to teach us biblical principles. Then, we must remember to be a doer of the Word, not just a hearer (James 1:22, KJV). A practical application is to take a Scripture that you are studying or meditating on and ask the Lord to provide opportunities to use His Word. Then, you must believe that He will provide opportunities which move you to a place of expectancy.

One day I was meditating on Proverbs 3:5-6: "Trust in the Lord with all your heart and lean not on your own understanding; in all your ways acknowledge Him, and He will make your paths straight." This was just what I needed because my car was malfunctioning, and I did not know what the problem was. I sensed that the Lord desired for me to use this Scripture to believe and trust that He would work things out. After acknowledging the Lord as my personal mechanic, I believed that He would give wisdom and knowledge to the person who worked on my car to discover the root cause of the problem. I also asked the Lord to give me favor by not allowing any unnecessary, costly repairs. I told the Lord that I would not lean on my own understanding by trying to figure out every minor detail of the situation.

We all know how we can get worked up at times while trying to figure out what the problem is, getting in God's way in the process. We need to remember that our understanding is limited and subject to error, whereas God is the all-knowing Alpha and Omega—the beginning and the end. Our understanding will never measure up to God's. The Lord reminded me that it is my responsibility to believe Him and His Word, and it is His responsibility to watch over His Word to perform it.

Satan, however, tried to put thoughts of doubt and unbelief in my mind to disconnect me from the promises of God, which prompted me to use another Scripture that has become important to me. Second Corinthians 10:5 says, "Casting down imaginations, and every high thing that exalteth itself against the knowledge of God, and bringing into captivity every thought to the obedience of Christ" (KJV). I've learned how to take negative thoughts captive and bring them to the obedience of Christ Jesus, allowing Him to be Lord in any particular situation. I then replace that negative thought with the Word of God and choose as an act of my will to submit to God and His Word. James 4:7 says, "Submit yourselves, then, to God. Resist the devil, and he will flee from you."

Notice in this Scripture that it says for us to first submit ourselves to God, and then resist Satan by refusing to accept his thoughts of unbelief. We must know God's Word in order to use it as a powerful weapon to pull down thoughts that are contrary to the Word of God. When we are not proactive in this area and don't pull down the negative thoughts, we allow strongholds to be erected in our minds.

This exercise of using God's Word allowed me to come into agreement with what he has said, not what Satan said or what my situation dictated to me. God is waiting to see if we will walk in agreement with Him, and Satan is also waiting to see if we will walk in agreement with him. It really is our choice. I decided to respond like Jesus and use the Word against Satan.

Now I manage my time to include practical application of the Word of God as directed by the Spirit of truth who guides me into all truth and shows me things to come through the Word. John 17:17 says that God's Word is truth. When I allow the Word of God to gain influence over my mind, there is a renewal that takes place, and I am able to believe what I could not believe before.

Making Time to Get Quiet Before the Lord

When I make time to get quiet before the Lord, it is intentional. I go to my listening room, a place where I won't be distracted by people or noise so I can be alone with God to hear Him speak to me. It is more than just a physical place for me; it also represents the condition of my heart. At first, I found that it was very difficult to focus on having my quiet time. The phone was ringing off the hook, and there always seemed to be something going on around me to distract me until I went before the Lord and asked for some help.

I told the Lord that I wanted to spend this quiet time with Him, but it was not working. The Lord spoke to my spirit, "Be still and know that I am God." That was enough for me. I decided to get my daughters involved whenever they were home and asked them to take a message if the phone rang. I told them that I needed their help in protecting my time with the Lord. The Lord put on my heart that this was a great opportunity to model before my daughters the value of spending quiet time with Him. Once I modeled this before them, I asked them to set time aside for the Lord so they, too, could learn to hear His voice and receive direction for their own lives. (It is always good to share our faith with our family.)

I would go in my bedroom and turn off the music or the TV, purposing in my heart to commune with the God of the universe. I had to literally set an appointment time with the Lord that would have no distractions or interruptions. Isn't that what we do when we have an important meeting with someone? Take note that when Satan sees that you are serious about setting aside time for the Lord, he will try everything in his power to distract you.

I also was distracted by the chatter of unnecessary thoughts in my mind. I had to go through the spiritual discipline of taking authority over my thoughts by ordering the voice of my natural mind to be quiet. I also had to take authority over Satan and command him to be silent in the name of Jesus, because he was trying to put his thoughts in my mind while I was quieting myself to listen to the voice of the Lord. Once I did this, I was able to be still and wait on the Lord. Remember, Jesus said that His sheep know His voice (John 10:14).

God will never speak contrary to His Word; therefore, if you hear any idea that contradicts His Word, you must cast it down and make it obedient to the Lord Jesus Christ and then replace that thought with Scripture. I will often go into my listening room with the Bible, so that I can read it in the presence of God.

I used to go into my quiet time anxious and concerned with the thought, *What if the Lord does not speak to me?* Instantly, I heard the Word of God spring up out of my heart with the answer to my anxious question: "Do not be anxious about anything, but in everything, by prayer and petition, with thanksgiving, present your requests to God" (Philippians 4:6). Then I relaxed, expecting to receive from the Lord. The Holy Spirit was really working with me to speak the Word of God to my heart. In every circumstance that comes up, we must yield to the Holy Spirit so that He will bring to our remembrance what the Word of God says. During this quiet time with the Lord, my spirit is communing with His Spirit through His Word, strengthening my relationship with His Son, Christ Jesus.

Hebrews 11:6 says, "For he that cometh to God must believe that He is" (KJV). This is the first thing that we must take time to do: believe that God is all we need Him to be. The rest of the Scripture says that we must believe that

He is a rewarder of them that diligently seek Him. For me to sow my time in seeking the Lord, I must believe both parts of this Scripture so that my investment of sowing will not be in vain. Now I am able to go into my listening room, ready to be quiet before Him and receive whatever He desires for me to have.

After spending many periods of quiet time with the Lord listening to His still voice, I know now when to be quiet and when to speak. At first, I would get quiet. When I sensed the Lord speaking to me, I got excited and started telling Him all about my day, the people who were bothering me, and what I needed. Then, I got quiet again, thinking that I just blew it. The Lord whispered to my heart that it is not all about me. Remember that communication is not a one-way dialogue, but rather a two-way dialogue. James 1:19, which tells us to be quick to listen and slow to speak, spoke to my heart. That was a very precious lesson for me to learn, and I am still working on it with the help of my family and friends who remind me to listen more.

How many of us go to God in prayer and do all the talking? The Lord desires to tell us some things that can change our actions and, ultimately, the course of our lives. He desires for us to be fruit-bearers by taking the time to cultivate an intimate relationship with His Son, Jesus Christ, in which we are connected to and dependent on Him, as the branch is to the vine.

John 15:5 says, "I am the vine; you are the branches. If a man remains in me and I in him, he will bear much fruit; apart from me you can do nothing." Jesus makes it clear in this parable that it is necessary for us to remain in Him and allow His life to be lived through us. If we are not arranging our daily schedule to get in His Word and His presence, then apart from Him we can do nothing that is pleasing to Him. This kingdom principle is foundational for understanding how we are to come to the Father in prayer through His Son Christ Jesus. I have discovered the importance of giving the Holy Spirit time to teach me these key truths from God's Word.

The Spirit will expose any untruths and guide us into all truth according to the Word of God. When we remain in Christ and His words remain in us, we can ask whatever we wish and it will be given to us (John 15:7). This is an important kingdom principle of prayer: we must pray to the Father in the name of Jesus, which means making requests based on His will that lines up with what His Word says.

First John 5:14-15 says, "This is the confidence we have in approaching God: that if we ask anything according to his will, he hears us. And if we know that he hears us—whatever we ask—we know that we have what we asked of him." Do you spend time with God and His Word so that you have confidence coming to Him, knowing that He hears you? Do you have a "common union" or communion with His Son, Christ Jesus, by abiding or remaining in His Word? We have to make time to spend time in fellowship with Christ and His Word and then exercise our faith.

Making Time to Use our Faith

When I take the time to get quiet before the Lord and allow His Word to saturate my thoughts, I experience a renewal of my mind that transforms me into the image of Christ. God then desires for me to respond in faith to Him and all that He is calling me to do.

Hebrews 11:6 says that it *is* impossible to please God without faith. The God-kind of faith is necessary for the believer to operate in the kingdom of God. This chapter begins with the practical application of the Word of God because faith comes by hearing and hearing by the Word of God. Remember that we need a steady diet of the Word of God going into our ears, through our eyes, and then coming out of our mouths with power. We all have been given a measure of faith, but now we need to make the time to exercise our faith.

The Lord once gave me a visual picture of me working out and looking fit. Learning from that image, I realized that if I do not physically work out, it does not amount to anything. That is how it works with our faith. It is good to imagine how we can use our faith, but faith without works is dead or inactive. Thus, I look for opportunities to use my faith as directed by the Holy Spirit.

I start my day asking the Lord to order my steps throughout the day, while confessing that I choose to walk by faith and not by sight according to His Word that I have hid in my heart to renew my mind.

When you believe God for things that line up with His will, then He will allow them to manifest according to His timing. The Lord will first give you opportunities to use your faith in small areas of your life. As you show faithfulness exercising your faith in the little things, He will give you opportunities to stretch your faith to believe Him for bigger things. Then, the Lord will take you to another level of glory in Him.

What I have found to be true is that the Lord desires that we not get complacent in our faith walk. Once, I asked my sister Jacquie if she wanted to agree in faith with me to walk in the supernatural with our faith eyes, believing that God would manifest His presence in the midst of our situation. She said no. I asked her why she wouldn't, because I was looking for someone who was operating in the same God-kind of faith that I was operating in. She told me that she felt that Satan would attack us more if we came into a higher level of faith. I reminded her that it did not matter anyway because as children of God, Satan hates us. Why shouldn't we be proactive and use our faith as a powerful weapon against his kingdom of darkness that has so many of our friends and family members bound?

After sharing with her about spending time in God's Word and getting in a place to be quiet before Him, she submitted to this spiritual discipline that has since transformed her prayer life and her faith walk. Now the two of us are looking for every opportunity to agree in faith on God's Word, believing that His power will be manifested in our midst.

The Lord is looking for believers who will exercise their faith so others will see the demonstration of His power and give glory to Him as the only true and living God. We all have seen powerful demonstrations of God's healing, deliverance, provision, and supernatural interventions in our midst. We just need to exercise our faith more, because God is able to make all grace extend toward us, giving us sufficiency in all things so that we may abound to every good work.

At one point in my life, I was struggling with my finances and only had a small amount of money to last until I got another paycheck. The Lord placed it on my heart to give the money to a friend who needed it. I had trouble with this because I could not see how I would make it if I gave the money away. The Lord desired for me to use this experience to exercise my faith, trusting Him to meet all my needs. I came into agreement with what the Lord had spoken to me and gave the money to my friend. She told me that she had believed God to provide for her financial needs and always found Him faithful. I began to weep because I realized that God had used me to bless someone else. Later that day, I received a check from an unexpected source that was ten times the amount of money that I sowed into her life. This small opportunity to exercise my faith stretched my faith to believe God in other areas that once seemed impossible for me to obtain.

The kingdom principle of sowing and reaping teaches that the seed you sow reproduces after its own kind. I sowed money and received money in return. If I sow acts of kindness, I will reap acts of kindness. If I sow my time into the kingdom of God, I will reap more time. If I sow food, I will reap food back into my home. On the down side, the same is true if you sow acts of unkindness, dissension, strife, or gossip. You will reap whatever you have sown in your life. Galatians 6:7 says that God will not be mocked; that which you have sown you will reap.

Time Management God's Way requires us to begin to think like God and take dominion over what He already gave us before the foundations of the world. I realize that my mind has its own limitations based on my physical environment, my past, and what the world dictates to me. When I get quiet before the Lord, there is a divine impartation into my spirit that helps me to receive any of the possibilities that exist in God. Any fear that tries to creep into my heart is silenced by the presence of the Lord. He often tells me that all things are possible to those who believe. Now I believe that He will reward me with all things that I can believe for. The capacity of what I can believe for is stretched to receive even more because of the power of God flowing through me.

Ephesians 3:20 says, "Now to him who is able to do immeasurably more than all we ask or imagine, according to his power that is at work within us." This is a powerful Scripture that the Lord desires me to meditate on, so that He can give me a fresh revelation of the truth of His Word to manifest later in my life. When I spend quality time with the Lord without any distractions, I can see with my spiritual eyes where He desires me to go and then allow the vision to enlarge in my heart before I walk it out.

Many of us cannot do what the Lord has planned for us because we have not spent the time necessary to get into His word and His presence. When we choose to make time to abide in Him, however, we will be saturated by the dew of His Spirit. The combustion of His fiery power will ignite us to become what has already been ordained for us before the foundations of the world.

Once, the Lord put on my heart to believe for returning the tithe to Him. This was a challenge for me because I was still recovering from financial difficulties. As an act of my will, I started where I was by being consistent in giving my offerings while I worked toward returning the tithe. Even though I was faithful in this area of giving, my heart's desire still was to tithe unto the Lord.

One day as I was spending a time of refreshing with the Lord, I told Him that I was $1000 short of my tithe for the year. I had come so far but was still short. The next day, a fellow believer gave me $1000 in cash and told me that the Lord had placed it on her heart to bless me with the tithe. I began to weep, seeing the faithfulness of God in this situation. The Lord recognized my desire to tithe as a seed and supernaturally allowed the seed to manifest. This increased my faith to believe God for more things. Today, I believe God for what will benefit His kingdom, not just for me. If we can just get a glimpse of how much the Lord wants to bless us with spiritual and material blessings, it would strengthen our faith in a mighty way.

Second Corinthians 9:10-11 says, "Now he who supplies the seed to the sower and bread for food will also supply and increase your store of seed and will enlarge the harvest of your righteousness. You will be made rich in every way so that you can be generous on every occasion, and through us your generosity will result in thanksgiving to God." The Lord will provide seed to the sower. The question is, do you have the lifestyle of a sower? Or do you just casually sow, not expecting the seed to produce a harvest as the Lord gives the increase? *Time Management God's Way* is based on the biblical truth of sowing and reaping—expecting God to increase your time to sow it back into His kingdom, not just to invest it in yourself

The only thing that counts is faith expressing itself through love (Galatians 5:6). God is love, and His nature resides in every born-again believer. When we allow our faith to be expressed through His love, we will begin to minister out of our love for God and obedience to His Word. As we are motivated by His love, then we will desire to spend more time with the King of kings and Lord of lords, looking for opportunities to walk by faith and not by sight so that His presence will be manifested throughout the world.

God will bless us with all we need when we make it our priority to seek Him first instead of the things of the world just to please ourselves. If our main focus isn't on God, we risk allowing the things of the world to capture our attention and become idols on which we lavish our affections. We also must be careful not to allow our affection for people to lead us to put them first in our lives. When we seek the kingdom of God and His righteousness, everyone and everything else will be set in its proper place.

At any rate, I continued to look for opportunities to use my faith in small areas of my life and then extend it to larger areas of my life. Because I desired to open my home for ministry, I believed God for a bigger house because my previous place had become too small. I told the Lord that with a larger house,

I could minister to more people in our small group ministry that was a part of our church. I desired to occupy a new home in my own neighborhood because during my prayer walks throughout the area, I had already taken spiritual dominion over it. The Lord laid it on my heart to proclaim the gospel and pray for the people in the neighborhood.

The developers, however, said that no more new houses would be built in the area. Even though at the time this looked like an impossible obstacle to overcome, the Lord reminded me of the Scripture that says all things are possible with Him (Matthew 19:26).

I had to repent of my limited way of thinking and ask God to forgive me, which He graciously did. I received faith to believe for this house, even when I did not qualify for a home in that price range. I did not share this hope with anyone until I allowed my mind to get a hold of the full revelation of God's promise to me.

The Lord put it on my heart to continue walking through the neighborhood to take dominion over what He had given to me. After several months, I did not see any change, so doubt and unbelief tried to slip into my mind. I told the Lord that I believed but to help my unbelief (Mark 9:22-24). All of a sudden, a sign for a new housing development went up in my neighborhood. The Lord had made it clear to me earlier that He would walk with me throughout this faith journey because I would soon have a testimony to share with others about my faith in Him.

The entire process of purchasing the house was a faith walk. God got all the glory when I testified to others of His faithfulness, His love, and His desire for us to walk by faith and not by sight. Many persons were blessed by my testimony of how good God is. There was an increase in the faith of many of my friends when they heard me tell them how I trusted in God to overcome the odds against me. Believing that God could bless them too, they began their own faith walk with the Lord. Now, they have their own testimonies to share.

The Lord taught me through this experience that He can make a way out of no way if we will only believe. He will give each of us opportunities to exercise our faith toward Him only if we believe that He is and a rewarder of those who diligently seek Him. We need to remember that the prayer of faith is based on God's will, which is His Word, and He will watch over His Word to perform it.

Making Time to Share My Faith with Others

Time Management God's Way requires the believer to share the gospel with whomever will listen. We do not know whose lives we will affect when we share the goodness of our Lord Jesus Christ. Romans 1:16 says that the gospel is the power of God unto salvation. I had become a witness to the saving power of God operating in my life.

In Acts 1:8, Jesus told His disciples that He desired for them to be His witnesses in Jerusalem, in all Judea and Samaria, and to the ends of the earth. As His disciples in today's world, we are to do the same thing by starting at home first. I discovered this to be true when sharing the gospel with my daughters. The Lord cautioned me not to hide my faith behind closed doors, but to openly share with them when led by the Holy Spirit.

I began to share with my daughters about my quiet time with the Lord and how hearing and obeying Him powerfully affected my life. The Lord reminded me that Jesus modeled His faith walk for His disciples so they could have a point of reference for what this faith walk looked like.

After I became consistent in my quiet time with the Lord, I asked my daughters, Selena and Shante, to spend about fifteen minutes of quiet time with the Lord without the TV or radio on. At first, my daughter Shante said it was the longest fifteen minutes she had ever experienced. She was right; I felt the same way when I started. Our culture is so busy and noisy that we are not used to silence. We usually want to turn something on for some background noise. Many people are missing a very peaceful encounter with the Lord when they do not seek Him in a daily quiet time.

At first, I did not even have to go outside my home to share my faith because I started with my daughters. Over time, their faith has increased as they heard my personal testimonies firsthand of my faith walk with the Lord. I asked them to submit to the spiritual disciplines that I had been practicing, while continuing to cultivate an intimate relationship with the Lord for themselves. I found it important to model my Christian values and lifestyle for them because the world was already dictating its values to them through TV, movies, books, and other people whose lifestyles were contrary to the Word of God.

I am not perfect, but I am constantly striving to be a doer of the Word and not a hearer only. What really blesses me is that both my daughters know that Jesus is the head of my home and that I choose to make the Word of God the final authority in my life. From time to time, they call me for godly counsel, and both of them will ask me these two questions: "Have you heard from the Father? Did He say anything to you about me?" My answer always is yes. They always call me after I have my time with the Lord. He often gives me a Scripture to pray concerning them personally or what they are going through at the time. I tell the Lord that if He wants me to speak to them about it, then He can prompt them to call me, and they always do. My daughters appreciate my words of wisdom over the phone because they know from watching me over the years that I value spending time with the Lord to receive His wisdom and guidance.

We can save time, money, tears, and frustration when we allow the Lord to teach us how to raise our children according to His Word and kingdom values. Will it prevent them from doing what they want? Not all the time. Proverbs 22:6 says to train up a child in the way (the Lord's way) they should go, and when they grow up, if they depart from the Lord's way, then He will bring them back. It's best to follow God's Word and instill Christian values in your children, rather than to let them do their own thing. When you do this, you can rest assured that God will do His part to remind them of His Word and teachings when they become adults. The Lord will never override their will, but His Spirit will convict them of sin in their lives and show them the right way to go.

I often encourage parents to take the time to train up their children in the Word of God when they are young instead of waiting until they become teenager or adults. If people would allow the Lord to teach them how to be better parents, it would definitely save them time.

One day, I was concerned about a decision that I had to make pertaining to my daughters, and the Lord spoke to my spirit to ask Him about it because He knew them long before I did. He reminded me that I may have carried them through pregnancy, but He had created them. He also showed me that he knows their thoughts before they get to their minds; in other words, He knows what they are thinking.

When we spend time with the Lord, His Spirit will reveal the truth regarding situations that we may know nothing about. We will be able to stand on the promises in His Word that can give us peace in the midst of a storm.

I took every opportunity to share my faith with my daughters so that they could develop the same spiritual discipline of spending time with God and His Word. They soon realized that He is no respecter of persons; instead, He is looking to see who will obey His Word and respond to Him in faith. My daughters have seen over and over how I depend on the wisdom of God by seeking His counsel through His Word for situations that arise. What better way to manage our time than by modeling godly values, along with our devotion and dependence on God and His Word, to our children!

Joshua 1:8 reminds us that when we spend time meditating on the Word of God, we will enjoy prosperity and success God's way in our lives. I often told my daughters to do their part by studying, meditating on, and then obeying God's Word; then they would receive His wisdom to live righteously and achieve the goals that He placed before them. In fact, when my daughters were challenged at times by their schoolwork, I told them to memorize and meditate on Scriptures to sharpen and renew their minds.

The Lord placed on my heart that children are a gift from Him. Thus, He desires for parents to raise them up in a Christian environment where they can see God's Word at work through their example. When they become adults, then we give them back to the Lord to continue walking with Him on their own.

When my daughters were young, I sensed that they were watching my walk with the Lord. Even as I started to tithe, for example, my daughter Shante said that she wanted to write out the check. As we use opportunities to share our faith with our children, they gain specific reference points of how the Lord honors His Word, which they'll remember later.

The Lord will show us areas where we can help our children to develop their gifts, talents, and abilities for Him while they are young, so they will have a desire to use them for His kingdom as adults. It is a blessing when you hear your children say that the Lord called them to do something and they are willing to do it. I often use my time to prophesy over my daughters and call those things that are not as though they are. As believers, we need to be proactive in speaking the Word of God in faith over ourselves, our family, and any situations that may arise. We should also allow our children to dream big because we do not know how the Lord will use them for His kingdom.

I had a conversation with my daughter, Selena, and she mentioned how the Lord showed her that He was going to bless her with financial wealth. I asked her to check her motives for using the wealth that the Lord would bless her with. She did not hesitate to let me know that she would tithe her increase and use the rest of her money to do the work of the kingdom as directed by the Lord. This truly blessed me because she is a giver who is motivated by the love of God operating within her heart.

In another situation, my daughter, Shante, observed my faith walk where I believed God for a debt-free car, and I received it. One day she overheard a conversation concerning the possibility that my car could be stolen and I should get a club to protect it. Shante spoke up and said that the same God that blessed me with the car is the same God that will send angels to protect the car. I never brought a club to protect the car. She had become proactive in her faith walk, and that really blessed me. *Time Management God's Way* is using your time to exercise your faith so that others, especially your family, might see your faith in action. The Word of God says that faith without works is dead.

Each of our children has their individual strengths and weaknesses. When we spend time with our God who knows the plans that He has for each one of them, He can give us guidance on raising them to be godly believers.

Sharing my faith with my daughters has given me the courage to share the gospel with my extended family, my church family, friends, and co-workers. The Lord gives us opportunities to use our faith in our comfort zones, but then He expects us to move into areas where we need to exercise our faith more.

As I look back over my faith walk with the Lord, I realize that my faith was very small, but now I am growing in my faith as I continue to study God's Word and apply it to every area of my life. You know when something good is happening in your life because you just want to share it. That is how it is with the goodness of the Lord. The Lord desires for each of us to take the time that He blessed us with to testify of His goodness to people that He brings across our path.

The Lord knows that I am looking for every opportunity to agree with another believer for the power of God to manifest in the midst of certain situations so that He will get all the glory that is due Him. He will give us opportunities to test our faith. The question is, are you exercising your faith muscle daily to receive more from the Lord?

Hebrews 10:38 says, "Now the just shall live by faith: but if any man draw back, my soul shall have no pleasure in him" (KJV). The Lord commands every believer to live by faith, and it isn't impossible for us to do. On the other hand, it is impossible to please God without faith. *Time Management God's Way* will require us to live by faith according to God's righteous standards and not to shrink back from using our faith in Christ Jesus, for that does not please Him.

Making Time for the Vision and Plans of God

When I take the time to spend quality time with the Lord to get His vision and plans for my life, I am truly blessed to see how the Lord orders my steps to walk out the blueprint that He has specifically designed for me. It is a time when I prepare my heart to receive the visions and plans that He has already established for me. In chapter 7, I shared a good portion of my testimony about how the Lord gave me a plan for my life and showed me how to carry it out. The one thing that has helped me to receive from the Lord is keeping a spirit of expectancy that the Lord has plans to prosper me and not harm me and also to give me a future and a hope. I do not know anyone else who can give me that kind of hope for my life; therefore, I am willing to seek God to find out what is important to Him and what is on His agenda for me. Once I decide to do this in my heart, God's grace is extended to me to do all that He calls me to do.

The Lord has directed me to set aside the first week of every month for Him so that He can prioritize any assignments or projects that He is calling me to do. During this time, I often fast as I'm led by the Holy Spirit, which attunes my spirit even more to His leading and guidance throughout the week. I also ask the Lord during this quiet time to give me any Scriptures that He desires for me to meditate on. When I receive these verses, I write them down in a notebook, along with any revelation pertaining to the Word given to me by the Holy Spirit. This activity is called journaling.

When I sit before the Lord journaling Scriptures or any insights that are given to me, I am in the right physical, spiritual, mental, and emotional position to receive from Him. This simply means that I am eagerly expecting to hear what the Lord has to say to me. When I receive a word from the Lord,

I may ask Him what it means for my life. The Lord may give me direction, solutions to a problem that I am dealing with, or answers to prayers that I have brought before Him.

The key to journaling is receiving what the Lord desires to speak to your heart. Often I re-read what I've written down and receive encouragement about how I am growing in the Lord. We may not have reached the place where we want to be in our faith walk, but we are also not where we used to be, which is a blessing. The Lord desires for us to continue putting our trust and faith in His Son Jesus, completely depending on Him to guide us through our lives while living a kingdom lifestyle that gives glory to Him.

Once I receive the plans and assignments that the Lord has given me to do, I come into agreement with them. I write down the vision of how the Lord desires me to walk them out by faith and then do them. Also in Chapter 7, I shared how I obeyed the Lord by completing the assignments He gave to me, no matter how small they were. When I proved faithful in those areas, the Lord opened the door for me to take on other assignments that helped me to develop character, perseverance, faithfulness, and commitment and allowed me to be responsible over what the Lord desired for me to do. When we are faithful over a little, then the Lord qualifies us to be faithful over much. This is a kingdom principle that requires the believer to submit to the Lord and not to skip over his assignment.

Whenever my schedule gets too busy, the Lord calls me to spend more time with Him. I have often decreased my time with the Lord, which is never good. Fortunately, the Lord will let me know how to prioritize my schedule to complete the assignments that He has called me to do. Then I can reduce stress, realizing that God is in control and has my best interests at heart. At times, I hear the Lord telling me to come away with Him, so I temporarily become a recluse to spend time studying and meditating on the Word. I try to create a spiritual atmosphere with praise music in my home that invites the Lord to come and dwell. Then, I can sense my spirit man being refreshed and highly sensitized to the Spirit of truth who will guide me in all truth.

During this "shut-in" time away with the Lord, I am usually prepared to receive divine impartations, visions, and dreams, along with fresh revelation from the Word of God. I come out of that time with the Lord ignited by the fire shut up in my bones, eager to do and become what the Lord was asking of me. This book was birthed out of a time of refreshing with the Lord. When I spent this kind of quality time with the Lord, I was able to see things from God's perspective more easily.

Some people may ask how I can take time to do this because I have a family that requires a lot of my time. Remember that the Lord will meet you where you are. I have not always been able to do this, but the Lord still keeps calling me to go higher with Him. He is the only one who knows the plans for our lives and what is required for us to accomplish these assignments. I have discovered that it is not enough just to start something if we do not plan to finish it as unto the Lord. The Lord will give us small steps to achieve the completion of the assignment or vision that He has assigned to us.

Once a year, I used to go on retreats with the church over the weekend to get alone with the Lord. Then, He asked me to take time off early on a Friday to spend some time with Him, because the home would be quiet. Eventually, I was able to use all of Friday as a day of rest to spend in the Word and in His presence. Each step of the way, I was coming closer to God, developing an intimate relationship with Him through His Word and through praise and worship. Now, the Lord revealed more of Himself to me, and I gave more of myself to Him, which is what a close relationship is all about. We should be able to spend intimate moments with the Lord and touch His heart with true worship.

The Lord helped me to cultivate this kind of passion by giving me opportunities to operate in childlike faith. It was difficult in the beginning because Satan did not want me to pursue this type of deep, intimate relationship with the Lord. I had to resist the attacks of distraction and hearken swiftly to the Lord's voice when He gave me directions on how to develop a single-minded focus on Him.

For example, the Lord may ask me to spend some time with Him over a period of several days going into the weekend. It may involve taking off work from a Thursday to a Saturday. The Lord will direct me to do all my chores from Monday through Wednesday, spending an hour on them each evening. Also, I will pay any bills or make any phone calls necessary to free my time up so I won't be interrupted by these distractions. This allows me to go before the Lord, free from the daily tasks that need to be done. When I hear the Lord tell me what to do, I am responsible to do it at the time when His timing is perfect and while His grace is operating for what is required. I was challenged in this area of obedience because I would often do what the Lord told me later than when He wanted.

The Lord spoke to my heart as a loving Father, admonishing me to obey Him by doing a task at the time that He asked me to do it. I found out that delayed obedience is disobedience. After learning this lesson, I am now quick to move when I hear the Lord speak to my spirit. I had to remind myself that much is required of those who have been given much.

We are always given opportunities to grow in our relationship with the Lord because He desires for us to accomplish all the plans and assignments that He has called us to do. He will not call us to do something that we are not prepared to do. The daily ins and outs of life provide opportunities to develop skills, discipline, and abilities to do different things. The Lord does not waste anything; instead, He allows all things to work together for our good that will ultimately yield good fruit in our lives.

I have learned to ask the Lord if my assignment is over. If He says no, then I know that His grace is still operating in my life to complete it. This has helped me not to be anxious about finishing a particular task that I know that the Lord has called me to do. If I have not spent quality time with the Lord to hear from Him pertaining to the start and completion of my assignment, then I may have allowed other people to influence my decision about it.

For example, many people have expressed anxiety regarding the timing of their retirement. I often ask them if they believe that their assignment is over. Some may say that they are sure, while others say that they are not sure. I counsel them to ask God to let them know if their assignments are completed. If they are not finished, then they are quitting before the Lord carries out His plan for them through their jobs.

Some people ask me if I am going to retire since I am eligible, but I say no because my assignment is not finished. I am not anxious or counting the days or hours until I can retire. I am content working where I am as unto the Lord until He tells me my assignment is over. The good thing about my dependence on the Lord is that He is preparing me to walk into my next assignment when I retire so that I won't miss a beat. It is awesome to know that I serve a progressive God who is always taking me from glory to glory in Christ Jesus. That is why He desires for me to manage my time according to His way, which is higher than my way of doing things.

I can continue to write about how the Lord is such a good time manager over my life, but I believe that I have given you enough practical examples of the way the Lord has guided me through the process of managing my time His way. The way to remember it is to yield your way to God's way because the Lord will never override your will. If you are a believer, then you can decide in your heart to sow your time into God's kingdom. Seek Him first to find out how He desires you to spend your time.

Remember that practical application of the Word of God is important to this process because it will illuminate your mind and help steer you down the right paths that will lead to your success. When you allow the Word of God to be your focus, then you will be able to strive after the things of God and not after the things of the world. This will help you to be Christ-centered instead of self-centered. Seeing things from God's perspective enables us to rise above our circumstances, troubles, trials, and limitations. *Time Management God's*

Way helps us take the limits off God and allow Him to do whatever He wants to do in our lives as we submit to His Word, His Spirit, and His way.

There is only one right way, which is God's way to live life. God is the giver of time. Because He knows the end from the beginning, He is the only one who can give us wisdom in how we should live our lives. People will know within their spirits that seeking God first for His counsel is the only way to live a godly, prosperous, and stress-free life.

If you are reading this book and are not a born-again believer, I hope that this material is a seed sown into your heart to prepare you to receive Christ Jesus as your personal Savior. God loved the world so much that He gave His only begotten Son, Jesus Christ to die for your sins and mine. When we repent and change our ways to return to God by believing on His Son, then we shall have eternal life.

If you have prayed for Christ to save you, all of heaven is rejoicing with you! You can begin your walk with the Lord who will help you manage your time better according to His kingdom principle of sowing into the kingdom of God and then reaping a harvest of bountiful blessings from His kingdom.

One last thought . . .

If you're not already attending a Bible-teaching church, ask the Lord to lead you to one that will equip you to do His work. May you know the joy of being in the right place at the right time, serving Him with all your heart.

ABOUT THE AUTHOR

Reverend Gloria N. Adams is a graduate of World Missions Bible College where she received a bachelors degree as an ordained minister in theology and biblical studies. Rev. Adams regularly teaches the prayer training class at the Bible Training Center, Win Institute, at Celebration Church—City of Champions in Columbia, MD. She is a small group ministry leader and participates in the Christian Guidance Ministry at Celebration Church. A devoted mother of two daughters, she is also part of the pastoral care program at Howard County General Hospital.

Rev. Adams has traveled and provided workshops for women's retreats, women's conferences and prayer breakfasts throughout the State of Maryland. A recipient of the Minnie B. Davis Faithful Women award from her church, Gloria is a respected role model for women in her church and community.

She has worked for the Food and Drug Administration as a chemist for more than 30 years since graduating from Howard University. Rev. Adams is the spiritual advisor for the Celebration Church School of Spiritual Dance and Angelic Steps dance ministries. She has researched and written 14- week semester syllabus and lessons for the dance school as well as workshops for the dance ministry at their annual retreat.

Rev. Adams is a freelance writer and member of the Baltimore Christian Writer's Group. Her poem, "Intimate Moments with Jesus," was published in the renowned National Library of Poetry, *The Other Side of Midnight*, which is a collection of poems.

Rev. Adams has a heart for the Great Commission to be taken around the world, wherever the Lord leads her. This passion for the lost and the needy has led her to become a missionary. She has taken several mission trips to Haiti, Trinidad, and Israel.

To Order This Book

This book may be ordered direct from the author. Send a check payable to GNA Faith Ministries in the amount of $12.95/book plus $4.00 shipping & handling/book, along with your name and shipping address, to the address below. If you desire an autographed copy, include the name(s) to be inscribed:

Rev. Gloria N. Adams
GNA Faith Ministries
8775 Cloudleap Court, Suite P 64
Columbia, MD 21045

410-884-7006 phone/fax
GloriaNAdams@aol.com
www.GNAFaithMinistries.com

Volume discounts available upon request from the author